MADE OF SALMON
Alaska Stories from The Salmon Project

MADE OF SALMON
Alaska Stories from The Salmon Project

NANCY LORD
editor

University of Alaska Press, Fairbanks

Text © 2016 University of Alaska Press

Published by
University of Alaska Press
P.O. Box 756240
Fairbanks, AK 99775-6240

Second Printing

Cover design by Jen Gunderson, 590 Design
Cover image and all interior images by Clark Mishler, *mishlerphotos.com*
Interior by UA Press

www.salmonproject.org

Library of Congress Cataloging-in-Publication Data

Names: Lord, Nancy, editor.
Title: Made of salmon : Alaska stories from the salmon project / Nancy Lord,
    editor.
Description: Fairbanks, Alaska : University of Alaska Press, [2016]
Identifiers: LCCN 2015022638| ISBN 9781602232839 (pbk. : alk. paper) | ISBN
    9781602232846 (e-book)
Subjects: LCSH: Pacific salmon fisheries--Alaska. | Salmon industy—Alaska. |
    Salmon—Alaska.
Classification: LCC SH348 .M25 2016 | DDC 639.2/75609798—dc23
LC record available at http://lccn.loc.gov/2015022638

The following essays were first published in the on-line *Alaska Dispatch*, in some cases in slightly different
forms: "Salmon Invictus," "Iqalugruaq: Chum Salmon and the Inuit World," "The Story Continues,"
"I Am Now the Age She Was," "Thank You, Swimmer," "Salmon are Worth More Than Money,"
"Seasons," "Size Matters," "Riversong," "Bristol Bay Youth Doing Their Part," and "My Salmon Project."

Development of the stories and essays in *Made of Salmon* was made possible by funding from the
Gordon and Betty Moore Foundation.

For the next generations, of salmon and Alaskans

Contents

Foreword

My earliest memories of salmon fishing are when I was a toddler, watching the subsistence nets to keep away the gulls. That was my job when we lived in Kanakanak, close to Dillingham. We had a good life. It was all about fishing.

Later, I was a commercial setnetter. My kids grew up fishing, and now my grandchildren are fishing. They put themselves through college. At the end of the commercial season, everybody goes upriver for subsistence fish. Everybody does the same thing, bears too. It's an incredible journey the fish make, and a wonderful system that, managed properly, will go on forever.

The years when I was Alaska's First Lady, going home to fish and visiting villages with Jay were my favorite activities. Everywhere, people were connected by salmon.

Today when my family comes to Lake Clark, we subsistence fish for our needs, and we smoke fish. My grandson built a new rack that is exactly the same as the rotted one his grandfather built years ago. I have a little radio I leave on all the time. Most of the conversation is about fish. It's fun to hear my neighbors talking about how many fish they caught and everything about fish. It's fun to watch the bears stroll by, looking for fish. I just can't imagine having a summer ever go by without fish.

When Jay was alive, politics was his territory. I left the heavy stuff to him. As governor, he used to talk about "battles between the buck and the biota," and it was uppermost in his mind to stick with the science and protect the future. But in recent years, I've had to take an interest in protecting our land and fisheries.

The people I converse with these days are more conservation minded than in the past. They want to take care of the environment. Politicians hardly use the word "conservation," which bothers me. Younger people are more conscious of the future, more aware of things that can be improved and are improving.

The voices in this beautiful book tell us of the many ways that Alaskans are grateful for the salmon in their lives and concerned for the future. All over the state, we're involved in different fisheries. We use different techniques, and we cut and prepare salmon differently. But we have salmon in common, and we know that we need to take care of what has served us so well.

Bella Hammond
Alaska's First Lady, 1974–82
Lake Clark

The Salmon Project

Salmon and Alaskans. We have danced with one another for millennia. For thousands of journeys around the sun, for more than three million spins of the earth, for hundreds of thousands of turns of the seasons, we have shared a rhythm. Each year, a great number of the hundreds of millions of salmon that mass and swirl in the currents of the North Pacific point their noses homeward and return to us. And we, in turn, move toward riverbanks, lakes, the ocean shoreline. We point our bows toward fishing grounds and travel to meet the fish on their return. As they surge toward us, we surge toward them. They help shape the rhythm of our lives.

The Salmon Project exists to tell the stories of the places and ways that Alaskans and their salmon come together. To help us learn about and see one another's salmon connections across the great distances of our state. To create the moment where we recognize our salmon-ness, and where we discover the bonds we all share—with the salmon and with each other.

Our salmon experiences are rooted in our home rivers, our family histories. In the landscapes where we have seen, harvested, heralded, mourned, celebrated, and welcomed home these beautiful creatures. We know the stream riffles and tiderips like the palms of our hands. Our young children can tell the difference between a chum and a coho. Our pantries are full of cans, our freezers of fillets and jerky. When we speak the word "salmon," an image comes up in each of our minds—of the river, harbor, setnet site, bay, rod, creek, deck of the boat—the place that is "home" for salmon in our minds, in our personal experiences. Try it now. Close your eyes. Speak the word "salmon." Where does it take you?

When we began The Salmon Project we hosted a series of a dozen focus groups in communities around the state. People came blind to the groups, not knowing that the conversation would be guided to salmon. They weren't selected because they had "salmon connections." They were pulled from the general population to meet basic demographic characteristics. Rooms full of strangers, often with very little in common, would warily enter into conversations about their values and what it means to live in Alaska. Eventually, salmon would come up, and the conversation would begin to follow that path. Invariably, the results were the same—in these rooms full of attorneys, teachers, young fathers, municipal employees, homemakers, retired professors, all would lean in. They would begin to share their own salmon stories. And they would paint clear, bright lines tying their values as Alaskans to the presence of salmon in their lives. Values connected to their families: "This is how my wife and I taught our children the importance of hard work." Values about freedom: "Being able to be out here, harvesting this resource, providing for ourselves." Values about culture and tradition: "My family and I have been coming to this beach every year for generations to harvest fish for the winter." And many more.

As we reviewed the results of this research, the thing that made the greatest impression on us was how quickly people could go from uncertainty about salmon's connection to their own lives to absolute engagement and realization of its role. An image emerged. It was that of "scratching the skin and revealing scales beneath."

We are salmon people. And what a blessing! How many other places in the developed world maintain seasonal rhythms tied to a living natural resource? Salmon nourish our lives and our spirits. In our research and engagements with Alaskans about salmon in their lives, one word comes up again and again—lifeblood. People find salmon so vital to their lives that to be separated from it would cause irreparable harm.

How are we doing with salmon in Alaska? The answer varies from watershed to watershed. We can look abroad or to the continental United

States and Canada for stories of devastation. We can look at our own fishery management and recognize that we're doing it better, that salmon still thrive throughout much of their range in our state. But we can also look at individual rivers, stocks, and systems and see that not everything is well. We know the value of our salmon, and we call it "lifeblood." But are we equipped to steward this resource for future generations?

With our connection comes responsibility. To sustain something as vital as our lifeblood, it is incumbent on us to know what it needs. We must understand the systems that support salmon and our role in influencing those systems. But equally important, we must recognize the place of salmon in our values. We must scratch our skin and recognize our scales beneath it. We must know that we are salmon people—not just in pockets around the state, but universally. We are the stewards of this resource.

And we must know one another. We must know that we are a team of hundreds of thousands of Alaskans tied to these fish. That we cherish them, and that they connect us all to our landscapes and to one another. That we all have "Salmon Love."

At The Salmon Project we've learned that many Alaskans know little about the salmon-lives of other Alaskans. Sometimes the very fact that we're so intimately linked to our own salmon in our own places means we miss the opportunity to see how they're married to the lives of others. We stay put in our favorite rivers, streams, and bays. Because it's salmon season! Too often our conversations about salmon in Alaska are rooted in conflict rather than connection. Too often we view others as people far away, over the horizon, who do not share our same values. We're so busy putting up our own fish, we never get to go to the place where others are doing the exact same thing. We teach our children to fish. We earn money for college. We work the fillet lines. We work the fly in the eddy by the turn in the creek. We make set after set after set in a seiner off a cape in a fierce gale. We feast. We have an idea that someone else out there might be doing the same thing, in some way. But we are worried about our stocks, our resource, the future, and we look for causes of harm everywhere but in ourselves.

This does no service to us, or to the future of salmon in Alaska. Our strength lies in our connectedness, in the roots that tie us to this resource. And our strength is in our shared voice—a voice that speaks for the resource, a voice that is raised in classrooms and community meetings, in advocacy and in story. Our strength is in a true understanding of this fish—its place in our lives and in the landscapes we call home. Not just spawning salmon in streams. Baby salmon. Eggs in gravel. The waters that sustain them. Adult salmon out in our great oceans. It is incumbent on us to know these fish and their needs, and to steward them. And in doing so, to steward ourselves. To allow a future in which our children and grandchildren enjoy the gift of salmon—and the gift of lives intimately tied to salmon's rhythms.

Alaska comes together with the returning salmon. We are united, a great mass of people living across a huge and stunning landscape, joined to one another by this beautiful creature who is born in our lands, travels away to the sea, and comes home. Bringing all of us along.

The Alaskans who share their stories, ideas, and beliefs in this book paint a picture of our shared Salmon Love. Through story, image, and conversation we will discover each other and the power of our shared resource. Together we'll discover a strong voice on behalf of our salmon—and our ways of life.

This book is a doorway into discovery. Join us. And begin your conversations.

Erin Harrington
Executive Director of The Salmon Project

Introduction

The other night my partner brought home part of a fresh king salmon fillet, gifted by a friend who fishes Kachemak Bay's winter kings and is generous with his catches. No matter that I'd already eaten dinner. "Yes, please," I pleaded, when Ken asked if he should cook a small piece for me.

I swear, there is no better food in the world than fresh-caught king salmon, grilled or broiled and with a little soy sauce. I ate that piece and then asked Ken for more. I would have eaten the whole side except Ken kept back a portion to take to an ailing friend.

This is the way of Alaskans and salmon. We share with one another; the fisherman divides his one or many fish among others, who cook or smoke or can and feed others, the circles widening through our communities. In our cases, the image of a circle expanding across the surface of water, perhaps from a leaping fish, seems particularly appropriate.

Alaskans, nourished by salmon in this way, are quite literally made of salmon. The protein, omega oils, and calcium pass from salmon into our bodies and bones, our good health. Beyond that, our families and friendships and communities are all made of salmon—through the ways we work together, eat together, and share not just salmon but common values.

Follow the circles out, and it's easy to see that Alaska itself, our home place, is to a great degree made of salmon.

Consider Alaska's indigenous cultures. The first people to inhabit our part of the world naturally chose the best places in which to live—those places defined as resource rich, where they had ample access to food. While some cultures oriented around sea mammal hunting and others around caribou, many of the first people were Salmon People above all, and most others, included salmon in their diets. Any glance at a contemporary map shows communities lined up on salmon routes—near the mouths of salmon rivers and streams and far into the Interior along salmon-rich rivers. Alaska's not an easy environment in which to live, and it's hard to imagine how there would have been much human success without salmon; salmon constituted much of Alaska's original wealth.

Salmon, for our indigenous cultures, were—and are—of course much more than food. Social organization, seasonal patterns, technologies, art, customs and beliefs, rituals, trade, warfare—all these and more were built in part on relationships to salmon. Today, as narratives in this volume will show, Alaska Native cultures maintain a deep and abiding connection to salmon and to values that developed alongside the shared use of salmon.

In the part of Alaska I'm most familiar with, around Cook Inlet, the Dena'ina Athabascans prospered along the major salmon streams. The Kenai Peninsula was called Yaghanen, or the "Good Land," in part because of its salmon strengths. Today around the mouths of the Kenai and Kasilof Rivers, and elsewhere through our salmon country, one can still easily find the outlines of semisubterranean Dena'ina homes and their associated salmon storage pits. For many years I fished on the west side of the inlet, near the old village of Kustatan, where I discovered similar hollows in the earth and imagined how it must have been for my predecessors to welcome each summer's returning salmon—kings, reds, silvers in turn.

Peter Kalifornsky, the Dena'ina writer and ethnographer, taught that in earlier times a day's food was a piece of dried salmon that reached from the base of your thumb to the end of your middle finger. He also documented the Dena'ina names for parts of a salmon—distinguishing among dried fish, half-dried fish, a bundle of dried fish, fish dried in one day's wind, fish dried with eggs inside, fish dried ungutted, fish dried flat, smoked fish, half-smoked fish, the backbone of the fish, the fish belly, the fat, the fatty part just in front of the king's dorsal fin, roe, dried roe, fermented roe, frozen roe, salted roe, and roe soup. Such a thorough and descriptive language attests to the central place of salmon in Dena'ina lives.

If Alaska was first colonized by foreigners seeking the skins of sea otters and fur seals, salmon were not far behind as a resource to be exploited. Salteries came first, then canneries. (By 1917, 118 canneries were packing more than half the world's salmon supply.) Barricaded streams prevented salmon from reaching spawning grounds, resulting in the rapid depletion of runs. Native people were kept from fishing their ancestral sites. Greed and waste abetted by a lack of law and enforcement made it seem that Alaska's great salmon runs would quickly become a matter of history.

Alaskans were rightly concerned about overfishing and federal misman-agement and were resentful of the cannery and fish-trap owners who con-trolled things from Seattle. (Fish traps, huge structures of fencing and nets, corralled migrating salmon into enclosures that could then be emptied onto scows and delivered to canneries, cutting out the need for fishermen and fishing boats.)

Salmon and Alaska's statehood are inextricably united. "Abolish fish traps" became a statehood rallying cry. When the push for statehood suc-ceeded in 1959, the new state of Alaska immediately banned fish traps and took over salmon management. The state constitution explicitly required "sustained yield" management for the state's fish and wildlife.

Take a look at the Alaska State Seal; a salmon swims around its outer edge.

As it turned out, traps themselves were not the conservation prob-lem, and statehood was not the solution. Fishing effort overall increased, employing many more Alaskans, and runs continued to do poorly.

But Alaskans again rose to the challenge and, in 1972, passed a con-stitutional amendment limiting the entry to salmon fisheries. Those with a history of salmon fishing were granted transferable permits, and since that time new fishermen can only enter a fishery by purchasing (or inheriting) an existing permit. The state also created a new fisheries division known as FRED—for Fisheries Rehabilitation, Enhancement, and Development— and undertook the construction of hatcheries and other pro-salmon projects. Then, the 1976 Fishery Conservation and Management Act (now known as the Magnuson-Stevens Act) established a system of federal fisheries management in the waters three to two hundred miles offshore, "Americanizing" our fisheries and bringing some controls to the bycatch and waste of salmon by foreign fleets.

Where once most attention focused on salmon as a commercial resource, today's Salmon Love is distributed more broadly, often in competing uses. Subsistence use (defined as "noncommercial, customary, and traditional") by Alaskans, historically so significant for Native and rural residents, is recognized as a priority use in state law. Sport fisheries have greatly increased, particularly connected to tourism, with king or Chinook salmon being highly prized. Alaskans also participate in personal-use fisheries to fill their freezers; the sockeye dipnet fisheries on the Kenai Peninsula, initiated in 1996, draw thousands of Alaskans every July. Many Alaskans participate in multiple forms of salmon fishing and depend on salmon for food, income, recreation, and, as many claim, "life." All five of Alaska's salmon species are considered fully utilized.

While Alaska's salmon runs are generally considered to be well-managed and strong, they face both on-going and new challenges. King runs have been in decline throughout most of the state, for reasons that are not well understood; necessary fishing closures have resulted in economic distress for many Alaskans and disrupted food supplies and ways of life. Offshore ocean trawlers continue to take (and waste) salmon as bycatch. Land-use and landscape changes, from urbanization to the construction of mines and dams, affect watersheds. Warming and acidification are causing significant changes to both stream and ocean habitats. Alaskans, in an increasing population, fight among themselves over allocations. The state of Alaska is in a fiscal crisis, which puts pressure on research and management budgets.

If only the right course to take in our new age was as easy as unblocking a stream.

I'm made of that king salmon I ate last night, and of all the richnesses of salmon that have filled my life. Ken and I made the decision as college students to move from New England, from which salmon had long disappeared, to Homer, Alaska, in part to be with fish. I have a photo somewhere of myself grinning over what might have been the first salmon I hooked on a line—an exhausted chum. Homer, in those days, was largely made of fish—the crab and shrimp fisheries as well as salmon. Among my first jobs were working in a seafood shop and the processing plant—the "cannery." Later, I worked for the Alaska Department of Fish and Game as a fishery technician at the Tutka Bay Hatchery, where we raised pink salmon for the common-property fishery and I made lasting friendships. I left that to become a setnetter—a way of life that Ken and I enjoyed for many years. More recently, I worked as a ship's naturalist and historian, teaching tourists about fisheries and fishing boats, taking them ashore to watch wild salmon spawning in wild creeks. Throughout my Alaskan life, I've written about salmon, fishing, and the natural world that embraces us all.

It was only a decade or so ago that I learned that the Amoskeag Falls that powered the industrial mills I'd grown up beside in Manchester, New Hampshire, were named from the Pennacook word for "good fishing place." The Native people there had once shaped their lives around the runs of sturgeon, alewife, and salmon. The thought of what was lost—what I never knew—breaks my heart.

We're pleased to present in this book heart-and-mind essays by twenty-one Alaska writers and thirty-four shorter "salmon shares" by other Alaskans. The essayists, after reading David Montgomery's landmark

King of Fish: The Thousand-Year Run of Salmon, were challenged to think about the role of salmon in their lives and our culture. The "sharers" were asked to show their salmon love. Clark James Mishler's artful photographs capture some of the faces and places that are, here in Alaska, "made of salmon."

Nancy Lord
Editor

A NOTE ON NAMES

Alaska's five salmon species go by a variety of names, differing by region and, in some cases, for marketing purposes. No effort was made here for consistency. Sockeye and red salmon are the same fish, as are silver and coho, king and Chinook, and pink and humpy or humpback. Chum salmon are also known as dog salmon, sometimes as calico or keta. "Alaska wild salmon" may be any species. Hatchery salmon (mostly pinks and considered "ranched") count among Alaska's wild salmon, but salmon farming (raising fish to market-size in pens) is forbidden by state law.

MADE OF SALMON
Alaska Stories from The Salmon Project

Salmon Invictus

LYNN SCHOOLER

Lynn Schooler, from Juneau, has been guiding professional wildlife photographers and natural history filmmakers around Alaska for twenty-five years. He is the author of *The Blue Bear*, *The Last Shot*, and *Walking Home*. Writing under the pen name Lynn D'Urso, he is also the author of the novel *Heartbroke Bay*.

IN AUGUST OF 2013 I was staked out on a river on an island in Southeast Alaska, waiting for a brown bear to come into camera range. The river was shallow and flowed clear as air over a bottom layered with speckled gravel and chunks of granite, some of which were large enough to create eddies where masses of chum salmon lay resting before heading upstream.

Everywhere I looked, dorsal fins flagged above the shallow water. Smooth, shiny backs rolled here and there, and now and then a hook-jawed head would rise above the surface to stare goggle-eyed at the swarm around it. The chum run was one of the biggest in history—some said *the* biggest—and the river was packed from bank to bank with fish. The conditions were ideal for protein-hungry bears.

But it was day two of waiting, and I had yet to see a bear, which was odd. I had been to the river many times over the past twenty-five years and couldn't recall ever spending more than a couple of hours on its banks during the peak of the salmon run without watching a grizzly swagger into the current to take its pick of the waiting fish. It was common to see half a dozen bears and sometimes more on any given day.

A few days earlier, a woman in a nearby village had mentioned that there was a rumor going around that the river was being evaluated as a possible site for a hydroelectric project. A valley upstream was ideal for a dam and the installation of turbines. A strip of yellow surveyor's tape fluttering from a branch gave some credence to the rumor, and I wondered if this could somehow have affected the bears. In Southeast Alaska, bears and salmon are as unshakably bound together as the atoms of oxygen and hydrogen in a molecule of water; it would take more than a few survey lines hacked through the brush to deter even a cautious bear from such an abundant source of food.

While I waited, I thought about what a dam might mean to the salmon and bears and the forest that sheltered them. The majority of the fish thrashing in the shallows would not be eaten by the bears, or the eagles, or the seals that waited near the mouth of the river. Most would spawn and then die and decompose, leaving only a few rags of skin and bone scattered along the banks and a lingering odor of rot, as invisible to the naked eye as the steady flow of their nutrients into the vascular system of the surrounding forest. The health of the watershed's entire ecosystem was as dependent on the annual arrival and dispersal of thousands of tons of marine-based nutrients as any Iowa cornfield is on the application of a farmer's fertilizer.

A power project would probably also mean a road, and studies have shown that a road of any sort almost guarantees that the brown bear population in a previously roadless area will drop by half, primarily as a result of increased hunting pressure. There would also be workers coming and going, helicopters churning overhead, and all the other activity that comes with development.

I pulled my thoughts back and tried to focus on the brush along the river. Two decades of filming and photographing wildlife had taught me that good photographs are usually the result of staying focused, patient, and, above all, persistent. Good nature photographers may wait days for the right moment of light and action necessary to capture a compelling shot; the great ones will pursue a particular image for years. Allowing a phantasmagoria of disturbing imaginings to draw my attention away from the river might mean missing a bit of motion in a tangle of salmon-berry bushes or some other small sign of an approaching bear. Besides, my mental distraction was based on nothing but a rumor and a few inches of yellow ribbon.

I was closing in on my sixtieth birthday, and I was tired of worrying about such things. From the time I was a teenager I'd watched as clearcuts, large mines, pipelines, and development projects had spread across the state like spilled oil. By now you're undoubtedly wondering what river I'm writing about, but the name of the river—or the inlet it feeds into or the island it is on—is of no particular distinction when it comes to a discussion of the future of Alaska's wild resources.

As I stood watching the chum swarm up the river, it began to seem as if every nurturing waterway of any consequence in the state had already been either significantly affected by human pressures or was under threat of compromise by the forces of big money and the pressing need for jobs and energy. The fish-rich Taku River, a few miles south of Juneau, is threatened by a mine development that would create millions of tons of acid-producing waste. The Pebble Mine, upstream of the incredibly rich Bristol Bay fisheries, could gouge a hole in the earth visible from outer space. And a seven-hundred-foot-high dam across the Susitna River is again under study.

I had begun to feel that any "victory" in the long struggle to preserve some portion of Alaska's irreplaceable wild resources was at best a simple holding action, and that the well-funded corporations that put a few quarters of opulent short-term profits ahead of centuries of consistent productivity were as relentless in their reach as the grinding of the earth's tectonic plates.

I was tired and burned out on the increasingly painful task of simply caring, and now all I wanted was to sit quietly by the river and listen to the ravens calling until I had a chance to photograph a grizzly. No more letter writing campaigns, or petitions, or meetings. No more feeling outraged by the shenanigans of politicians ever willing to rewrite existing laws and regulations to please big campaign contributors and industrial lobbyists.

Then something odd caught my eye. Amid the swirling mass of salmon finning along a bend that took the river out of sight upstream, a single salmon appeared, drifting slowly downstream. A bright red wound gaped on its back. Every few yards the fish would right itself and begin swimming desperately, pushing its way back up through the crowded water, muscling into the current in spite of its injury, until exhaustion rolled it onto its side and it begin floating downstream again. It swam, gave up, and then flopped over and washed downstream, only to rise, swim, and repeat, over and over again.

As the fish drifted past me, gasping and chopping its jaws at nothing, I could see that the wound on its back formed a deep *U*—a missing hunk the size and shape of a bear's mouth. Somewhere out of sight upstream, a bear was feeding, sampling bits and pieces of individual fish before dropping them and moving on to the next.

It was both heartbreaking and awe-inspiring to watch the wounded fish, bitten down to the spine, with the bulk of the muscle between its head and dorsal fin gone, struggle to get back upstream, driven by eons-deep genetic programming. I had never seen a creature so hell-bent on procreation.

After a final flurry of effort, it rolled onto its side and drifted slowly downstream out of sight toward the inlet. I watched it go and then pushed aside the small bloom of melancholy that had begun to form in my chest and forced myself to focus my attention upstream again, where I was now certain a bear was feeding.

Nothing happened. An hour passed. Then another. The tide changed and began swelling up from the inlet into the mouth of the river, climbing the banks, changing the musical tones and scales of water flowing over stones in the river until silencing them altogether as the streambed filled and grew still at the top of the tide.

A fresh wave of salmon moved in with the tide. In the relatively short streams and rivers that fall out of the mountainous islands of Southeast Alaska, the metamorphosis of chum salmon from silver-bodied bullets into goggle-eyed, gator-jawed beasts clad in vivid red, green, and yellow stripes happens much quicker than among the runs that make long journeys up rivers like the Yukon or the Nushagak. The new arrivals were easy to spot among the early fish in their Jacob's coats of bright colors.

Watching the pulse of new fish move upstream was like watching a heart beat, like seeing the lifeblood of everything that grows in the forest flowing through the veins and arteries of the planet. It was getting late, the shadows along the banks were growing dark with the approach of evening, and my mind settled the way the rising tide had quieted the river.

And then it was there again—the wounded fish, the terrible gape in its back gleaming red and tattered. It was upright and moving slowly, pushing forward a foot at a time. It's strange to feel sentiment toward a fish, but its determination made my throat catch. In a few minutes it had pushed out of sight upstream.

It struck me then that such determination is precisely what it will take to keep Alaska's rivers full of wild salmon. In the face of ever-increasing threats, it will take Alaskans who care enough about their traditions and livelihoods, and the health of wild fish populations, to keep organizing, writing, attending, petitioning, demanding, and refusing, even when the sheer size and power of the forces gnawing at the wild runs make it feel as if the back has been bitten out of the average Alaskan's power to affect things. It may take generations of such single-minded determination to do so.

It was late and I had already started gathering my things when the bear materialized out of the growing shadows across the river, appearing on a gravel bar a hundred yards upstream. It was too far away for a photo, and all the color was gone from the scene, and as I watched, the bear became nothing more than a dark shape moving slowly along the edge of the river. So I shouldered my pack and started walking. I knew I would be back again. If I really wanted that photo, I'd just have to keep trying.

My fishing heritage started when my great-grandfather Sigurd Aardal immigrated from Norway to Washington State. He was an innovator, and his was the first commercial salmon vessel to use an engine in the Puget Sound area. My father, William Connor, felt the calling at the age of seventeen and, with nothing but a sleeping bag and forty dollars, made his way to Alaska. His story is rich and colorful, but it is not mine to tell. However, if not for his sense of adventure and love for fishing I would not be the man I am today. I learned from him a sense of pride, respect, and hard work that has seen me through the harshest of times—from growing up poor, to combat tours in the Middle East, to battling multiple sclerosis, and finally scrimping and saving enough to buy my own boat for the Bristol Bay drift fishery. There have been many times I wanted to give up, but that childhood of hard work and never-say-quit attitude always drove me to put that next foot forward. Maybe it is in the blood, maybe it is my father's and mother's great parenting, or maybe, as I like to think, it was the sight of that first shiny salmon wriggling in my hands when I was just a young boy.

Dustin Connor
Petersburg

"Do you have any fish?" the woman on the telephone asked. I felt irritated. It seemed like I was always getting phone calls from people asking things of me. People wanted to borrow tools, which often didn't get returned. Money. Babysitting. Now fish.

I pictured the two salmon in my freezer. It was the end of winter. Spring thaw was just around the corner. I thought of the river and how, year after year, the fish generously travel up the silty glacier water and offer themselves to the people, the bears, the eagles. I thought of the shallow branch of the river that kindly curved toward my home. I envisioned the splashing of the waters as the king salmon thrust themselves over the rocks, toward the mouth of the creek that dumps into the river. A wave of love washed through me.

"Come over," I told the woman on the phone. With a heart full of grace and a smile on my face, I gave her the last of my fish.

Later that day, I went to the river, to the place where the water was open, and I made offerings to the salmon people. I prayed that their journey be well. I thanked them for their beautiful bodies, full of nutrients. I felt shame as I thought of how generously the earth gives, and how I had become stingy with my time and resources. I let the shame pour out of me and travel down the river. I vowed to be more generous, more open and flowing. More like the river.

That summer, when the ice moved out and the salmon moved in, I approached the fish differently. I was mindful of my mood as I processed the fish that I got from a neighbor's wheel. I allowed awe a place at the outdoor butchering table, and my hands touched the fish with gratitude. They were no longer just a food source. They were like family.

That year, and the following three years, I received generous gifts of fish from people. One man brought me a large cooler full of fish, already gutted. He was the husband of a woman who despised me. I looked at the orange and red flesh of the salmon, and I thought my heart would burst with joy. In my mind I pictured my enemy, and I extended my overflowing love to her. The river excludes no one.

The salmon taught me about grace. They taught me about generosity. They taught me humility. The Ahtna people, who had relations with the salmon long before me, say that one should always bathe before touching the first salmon of the season. It is an act of respect. I don't think it is necessarily about body cleanliness, though. Maybe it's like the Christian baptism, or the Jewish bath, that is more about spiritual cleanliness.

I was called to the altar by a woman on the line, and there I was baptized by glacier water and salmon slime. It set me right.

Chantelle Pence
Chistochina

Iqalugruaq: Chum Salmon and the Inuit World
WILLIAM L. IGGIAGRUK HENSLEY

Willie Hensley is the Distinguished Visiting Professor in the Department of Business and Public Policy at the University of Alaska Anchorage and serves as chair of the First Alaskans Institute. His career includes service in the Alaska State Legislature and state government, in many roles with the Alaska Federation of Natives and NANA Regional Corporation, and most recently in government relations for Alyeska Pipeline Service Company. He is the author of *Fifty Miles From Tomorrow: A Memoir of Alaska and the Real People.*

WHEN I WAS A BOY IN QIKIKTAGRUK (KOTZEBUE) in the 1940s and 1950s, our world still revolved around the seasons and the natural rhythms of the resources that sustained us. We were still completely dependent on our dogs for transportation during the long winters. The hardwood sleds that were crafted by hand were works of utility and art. I remember men hand cutting the hardwood with saws and the effort to steam the wood to make the curves for the runners and the decorative oval hoop for the back of the sled.

The winter was a time of trapping for wolverine, wolf, land otter, fox, lynx, and ermine. We set our nets under the ice for *shi* (sheefish). We set hooks in the rivers for *tiktaaliq* (ling cod). We hunted rabbit and ptarmigan and caribou.

In the spring, the migratory birds came to break the monotony of rabbit, ptarmigan, and white fish in our diet. Now there were ducks and geese and swans and eiders. Spring also was the time for hunting muskrat, which brought a nice price at the trading post so we could pay down the debt from the winter and perhaps buy more equipment for hunting—even a new motor or boat or rifle. Spring was also a time to replenish the seal oil barrel—an absolutely necessary source of energy and nutrition. The oil preserved the dried seal meat, the dried fish, and the cooked seal intestines. The seal oil in traditional times was food, heat, and light.

Summer was the time to prepare for winter. It was a busy and frenetic time to insure a huge supply of protein for both man and animal. Beluga provided dried meat and the *maktak* (prized skin and fat, known in English as muktuk) that was stored in pokes made of the seal's own skin. Then there was the run of *iqalugruaq* (chum salmon) that was critical for the coming winter.

The three-mile-long beach of Kotzebue was a beehive of activity in the summer. Here the family *inisiaq* (meat/fish rack) was erected of spruce trees and driftwood to dry the salmon and other products for preservation and storage. Every home used the beach extensively for butchering beluga, seal, walrus, and salmon. Here they dried and cooked and stored the food. Here they took the sealskins and used the ulu to scrape the fat and tissue and stretched the skin to the ground using wooden pegs and a small pole. Later the women would use the *ikuun* (scraper) to begin the final transformation of the skin to be used for mukluks, parkas, mittens, and warm pants for the winter. Or the men might take a sharp knife and tediously cut the skin into a thin rope that could be used for making sleds or to tie down the loads or as straps for the rifles.

The women would make a fire to cook the beluga muktuk and half-dried beluga meat. They would also make *mukpauraq* (homemade doughnuts). The children would sit around in the grass making themselves conspicuous, hoping for a hot, tasty treat. They were most often rewarded.

Iqalugruaq were critical to Inupiat survival back then. Your family needed the food, and, importantly, your dogs needed sustenance as well.

Kotzebue was well located as the salmon came through the shallow channels from the Bering Sea and into Kotzebue Sound. The primary channel extended from the beach a few hundred yards to the shallow, silt-laden waters deposited by the Noatak and Kobuk Rivers.

By Bristol Bay and Yukon salmon run standards, the Kotzebue chum run is rather small. But in the lives of the people, it is very significant. In the dog-team days, one family would be required to catch, butcher, hang, and dry at least a hundred bundles of salmon to keep the dogs fed during the winter months. Each bundle contained at least twenty-five salmon. So there was a need for at least twenty-five hundred salmon to be put away. Any extra bundles would be used for trade with others or for sale to the traders to buy essential items for the coming year—rifles, sacks of flour and sugar, oats and coffee, tea and ammunition as well as traps and Coleman lamps and Primus stoves.

Kotzebue people didn't need to smoke salmon in those days. Smoking takes time and energy. You had to build a smokehouse, cut the salmon into strips, cut the alder, and tend to the smoking. With drying, we had nature to help us. We had a stiff west wind that blew almost constantly at fifteen to twenty miles an hour, and that wind turned the salmon into firm, storable protein that was very tasty with seal oil or blubber for humans and easily handled, lightweight food for the dogs on long trips. If the weather didn't cooperate, the flies would lay their eggs and the boys would have to go through each and every hanging salmon to make sure there were no *qupilgut* (maggots) on them. Once in a while the qupilgut might fall into the neck of your shirt if you weren't careful. Other times, you would build a nice smoky fire with green grass and weeds to keep the flies away and the qupilgut would drop to the gravelly beach.

The canned salmon industry, in the early days, was rapacious. They virtually privatized the salmon in Southeast Alaska with the fish traps, literally taking food out of the mouths of the Tlingit people who depended on the fish for their sustenance. There was even a cannery in Kotzebue, built at the turn of the twentieth century. We were, in a sense, at the end of the salmon food chain. We didn't have the variety of salmon caught farther south, and only occasionally did a king salmon enter our nets. The cannery in Kotzebue eventually went out of business, but in later years, when the airplane became an everyday occurrence, the commercial salmon industry took root and our people began to fish for cash.

It was nothing like the giant commercial fisheries in Bristol Bay, the Gulf of Alaska, or Southeast Alaska, but it was a fishery that did provide residents the opportunity to earn cash to buy items of value in their daily lives. The commercial fishers in Bristol Bay were accustomed to very expensive permits and vessels and crews for their livelihoods. Our Kotzebue Sound fishermen used small outboard-powered boats and fished by themselves or with their sons or brothers. A $10,000 summer would be a big year for most fishermen, but occasionally they earned $20,000 to $45,000 in high years.

We didn't have the "fish wars" that became part of the normal political scene elsewhere when commercial, sport, and subsistence users battled for their particular uses.

Life has changed dramatically in all of Alaska since statehood. In rural Alaska, the changes have been extensive and in some cases traumatic. Every area of life has been affected by modernization. But when summer comes, people take the time to set their nets, enjoy the millennia-long pleasure of putting up fish for the winter, work with their families, and appreciate the bounty of nature. Iqalugruaq, the salmon, has always been a part of our annual cycle.

In 1967, while I was living in Juneau, my friend Pete Hansen invited me to go king salmon fishing. Having never fished with Pete, or for kings, I had no idea what to expect.

For hours, we trolled herring around Auke Bay in Pete's small skiff. Nothing. The light was fading, as were our hopes. Then something yanked the tip of my rod down.

Until then, the biggest fish I'd ever hooked was a five-pound humpback salmon. This fish felt much heavier than that. It pulled hard, heading for the bottom, taking line. I was lucky it didn't run far, as my spinning outfit wasn't up to handling a big fish. The fish twisted and turned near the bottom, jerking its head against the pull of my line. When it finally stopped struggling so hard, I pulled as hard as I dared and slowly regained line.

I've never been so excited as when that big, silvery fish swam into sight from the depths. It turned on its side, and I led it into Pete's landing net. I'd never seen anything so perfect and beautiful. It weighed thirty pounds.

It was dark by the time Pete and I came in, so I gutted the fish in my apartment. It took up most of my kitchen counter. When I cut into it, I saw that its flesh, instead of being red, was white. I'd never heard of such a thing. Concerned, I called Pete and told him about it.

"Yah, some are like that," he said. "There's white kings and red kings. You caught a white king."

"Oh. There's nothing wrong with it? It's good to eat?"

"Oh, sure. You can't tell the difference."

He was right about me not being able to tell the difference. I'd never eaten red king, let alone white. Still, to this day, I remember that king as the tastiest, prettiest, fightingest salmon I've ever caught.

Les Palmer
Sterling

The Story Continues

SARA LOEWEN

Sara Loewen received her MFA in creative writing in 2011 from the University of Alaska Anchorage. Her first book, *Gaining Daylight: Life on Two Islands*, was published by the University of Alaska Press in 2013 and won the 2014 WILLA Award for creative nonfiction. She teaches at Kodiak College and fishes commercially for salmon each summer with her family.

> *This land, this water, this air, this planet—*
> *this is our legacy to our young.* Paul Tsongas

OUR SIX-YEAR-OLD WASN'T HAPPY about leaving the fish site this fall. What kid wants to give up daily skiff rides and building beach fires and driftwood forts for alarm clocks and classrooms?

To ease his reluctance, I let him pick out his first real fishing pole when we were back in Kodiak. His little brother, Luke, inherited the rusty push-button rod with Star Wars sound effects that no longer casts but was still good for poking at things.

Grandpa wasn't sure that Liam was ready to bring in a silver, and it's true I spent a good part of our first trips to the river untangling his hook from alders and steering Luke and the dogs away from his erratic casting.

But when Liam backed a bright twelve-pounder onto the gravel, and we drove that silver straight to Grandpa's, and when, every day during journal time for the first month of first grade, Liam drew fishing scenes,

I could see the river, the flight and fall of each shining lure, the beauty of those salmon, the praise over dinner all becoming a part of my son's story.

For the remainder of the fall, after school and every weekend morning, Liam begged to be taken fishing. And often we went, even though it meant lifting our old lab into the bathtub to wash off the slime and stink of rotting humpies he'd rolled in. And drying out Luke's boots over and over. Or wading out on a submerged tree, seven months pregnant, way over my boots, to untangle his lucky lure.

As parents, we want the stories that shape our children's lives to be made of good things—effort and success, nature and wonder.

For many young Alaskans, salmon are already a part of the seasonal rhythm of each year through subsistence, community, or commercial fishing. That may be exactly what the future stewardship of Alaska's wild salmon depends on.

Salmon "embody our home places," writes Tom Jay, the Pacific Northwest sculptor and writer who has long celebrated salmon in his work. "Salmon are the deep note of our dwelling here."

I've watched our boys' attachment to our setnet site on the west side of Kodiak grow with every season. To see it is to glimpse my husband's childhood here—what made Peter the man he is, why he defines himself through this work and place.

Kodiak setnetters pick salmon one by one, pulling each fish from nets stretching 150 fathoms into the ocean. How many thousands have passed through Peter's hands?

From a mile across the bay, he recognizes reds or pinks or dogs by the shape and path of their leap. He knows salmon in a way I never will, though they are the calendar around which we arrange our year—moving to the cabin each May and returning home in the fall. Salmon are our mortgage payment, the food in our freezer, peace of mind in good seasons, and worry in the lean ones.

While I was growing up, our family spent September afternoons fishing in Barling Bay, near the village of Old Harbor. At six or seven years old, I preferred to set down my fishing pole and tried instead to usher dying salmon back into the river. "There you go, little fellow. You're free. Live, live," I'd urge each gaping, decrepit fish as it floated off sideways into the current.

Sometimes when I consider what I can do about climate change and ocean acidification and its impact on the future of wild salmon, I feel about as effective as that little girl.

Will depleted, warmer oceans continue to support a species so dependent on open ocean feeding and specific water temperatures?

Salmon runs have been declining and disappearing across the globe for the last thousand years, though no one actually sought to destroy them, writes David Montgomery in *King of Fish*. "Decimated salmon runs resulted from individual and collective greed, negligence, and indifference, together with the cumulative impact of human activities that gradually degraded the ability of the land to sustain salmon."

Has Alaska—one of the last great strongholds for healthy stocks of wild salmon—merely delayed the sort of loss that has occurred in Europe, New England, California, and the Pacific Northwest?

"What does it mean to be alive in an era when the Earth is being devoured, and in a country that has set the pattern for that devouring? What are we called to do?" Scott Russell Sanders asks in *Writing from the Center*. "We can begin that work by learning how to abide in a place. I'm talking about active commitment, not a passive lingering."

We know that clean, undamaged rivers and streams are vital for healthy salmon returns; history has shown that no amount of hatchery effort can fix runs destroyed by ruined habitat.

While Alaska's remoteness and small population seem to have spared our salmon the fate of so many other Pacific salmon runs, is our fidelity to wild spaces, and our long knowing of salmon within these places, enough to compel the "active commitment" that will keep Alaskans vigilant?

Of the fifty states, only Alaska commits in its state constitution to managing natural resources like salmon for a sustained yield. This foresight at statehood was based on the belief that replenishable resources should be managed not for maximum short-term economic gain but for perpetual gain.

We can advocate for salmon by asking that our political leaders, stakeholders, and fish managers protect our wild salmon populations and habitats, especially with growing pressures to extract resources from salmon watersheds as oil revenues decline.

We deliver our fish to a cannery that's been there since 1910. People have been harvesting salmon here for millennia. At fish sites around Uyak Bay, a third generation now picks nets alongside cousins, parents, siblings, and grandparents. You find this all across our state—extended families working together and sharing a resource—and seeing it makes tangible the idea of conserving salmon runs to leave a legacy for our young.

In *A Sand Country Almanac*, Aldo Leopold wrote, "We grieve only for what we know."

Those fall mornings, well before sunrise, when I fix Liam's lunch and he dresses in the dark so as not to wake his brother, we whisper good-bye, good luck, and he picks up his beloved tackle box, grabbing the hand of Papa or Grandpa waiting at the front door—I cry every time, at the sweet circular blessedness of it all. I don't want to grieve for lost salmon runs.

I know salmon as a livelihood, and as part of this fishing community, but also as some of my best childhood memories—wading through sharp green beach rye into open, bear-trampled spaces, where my footsteps sent the glint of tail or fin dashing out from the cover of a riverbank, and Mom handing out sandwiches and passing around a thermos lid of Russian tea to warm us up after a long cold skiff ride.

Salmon are the story of both my birth family and the family I've made. They are incentive for living a life that is materially simpler and raising children with an ecological conscience.

When we drove out to the American River on a Sunday morning in December, it was a different river from the one we visited so many times in the fall, when Liam was caught up in the fervor of fishing, envying the grownups' waders, and looking earnestly for a glimmer of silver within crowds of mottled pinks. Now we were alone—no lines of fishermen along the banks or rows of trucks with coolers ready on the tailgate.

The road was quiet, the sunlight between mountain shadows slanted and butter pale. It was just starting to snow, and the river mirrored the metallic luster of low clouds. By midwinter, such rivers are generally far from our thoughts.

"You remember all those humpies that were spawning here in September?" Peter asked Liam. "All those eggs are in the river now, and in the spring the pinks will migrate out to the ocean, even though they'll only be an inch long. They'll head out like a fleet of tiny submarines."

Liam nodded, but he was more interested in an old lure he'd spotted snagged on a logjam.

There are plenty of years to bewitch him with science—scientists estimating historic runs by trees in Southeast Alaska that grew faster in years of abundant salmon, or the feats of homing and imprinting that guide salmon back to natal streams.

Walking with our boys beside the river, I think of our biggest commitments—joining in a marriage, raising children, choosing to call a place home—and the sanctuary of this river, hiding millions of salmon beneath still water and gravel, and the work of tending to and protecting what we love.

I hated going down to the net throughout my teenage years, facing many cold, windy, rainy nights. But now that I'm older and have a chance to reflect on those memories, I remember waking up to a gorgeous Bristol Bay sunrise with the smell of pancakes in the air. I would walk out on our porch to feel the cool breeze kiss my face. The beautiful golden rise of the sun would dance on the water, glisten off the whitecaps. Fishing boats would pass by our cabin as they were on their way to drop off the early morning delivery.

These are the moments I reflect on. These are the memories I treasure. Fishing is about making a life. It is a tradition to pass down to my kids. Splitting fish, making strips, canning fish are all about the way of life. It's what my grandmother did with her family each summer to provide for the winter meals. Going down to fish camp now is about keeping my roots alive and passing traditional values and culture down to my children. Mending nets can be tedious work, but the gratification mends the soul.

This culture runs in my blood, in my bone, in my heart, and in my spirit. I love my tradition of fishing, and I write this to share the passion with you. Every fish is a blessing, a good meal, and a constant reminder of how my family has lived for generations.

Heidi Hurley
Anchorage

I can think of no one who loves to fish for salmon more than me. I will be the first one on the river in the spring as soon as the ice is off and the last one fishing for salmon even when we get the first snowfalls of the season. I fish in all kinds of weather for hours on end.

Back in 1983 I caught a sixty-eight-pound king salmon on the Kenai River, and from that moment on I have tried to catch one bigger. In the meantime I count the days in winter until I can get on the river or ocean to start fishing for salmon. I fish daily when I can, and when I can't I think about fishing for salmon. I prepare my various tackle boxes with new gear for the following season. Ask anyone I know and they will tell you how obsessed I am about and with salmon. It is what keeps me going in the winter months and what keeps me going in the summer.

I am sixty-three years old, and I hope to live a long life, but as I have told my children, the last thing I hope to be doing on this earth is fishing for salmon. If that isn't salmon love, I don't know what is. My grandkids call me the "Crazy Grandma," and when no one can reach me, they already know where I am and what I am doing.

I am ready to go fishing. Any takers?

Juanita Dwyer
Wasilla

Ship Creek is a favorite urban fishing spot near downtown Anchorage, in the industrial port area. King salmon peak in June, and a fishing derby benefits the local soup kitchen.

Subsistence-caught salmon contribute both nutritionally and culturally to Alaskan life. The Nushagak, here seen near the village of Ekwok, is one of two main salmon rivers in the Bristol Bay region.

Tenders—like this one on Nushagak Bay—transport salmon from commercial fishing boats to processors. Here high-valued king salmon have been separated from a setnet catch.

(Top): The Kenai River, on the road system close to population centers, is the most popular sportfishing destination in Alaska. King, sockeye, and silver salmon arrive in separate runs throughout the summer.

(Top left): The Bristol Bay sockeye salmon fishery is the world's most valuable wild salmon fishery. In 2010 Bristol Bay salmon fishermen harvested twenty-nine million sockeye salmon worth $165 million in direct harvest value, and the fishery supported twelve thousand fishing and processing jobs.

(Bottom left): The Wood River connects Nushagak Bay to a salmon-rich lake system. Here, close to Dillingham, it's at its widest.

Systems for cutting and drying subsistence salmon differ by village and family. This drying rack is at a fish camp near Kwethluk, just upriver from Bethel in western Alaska. The Kuskokwim River is home to the largest subsistence harvest of king salmon in Alaska.

A variety of boat types serve as tenders to transport salmon to processing facilities. This one was serving the seine fleet near Ketchikan. Tenders keep fish chilled with either ice or refrigerated seawater.

For years canning was the primary way of preserving salmon, and canning lines such as this one in Ketchikan still operate. Today salmon is largely sold as fresh and frozen product, but canned salmon remains a staple in parts of the United States and in England.

Family Business

CAROL STURGULEWSKI

Carol Sturgulewski is a lifelong Alaskan who has lived in nine communities all over the state, from Fairbanks to Dutch Harbor to Wrangell. She has written and edited newspapers, books, and magazines in Alaska for more than thirty-five years and cannot imagine a better life. She and her husband, Roe, now live in Anchorage.

"HE'S DOING GREAT," the pediatrician said, handing back my hefty three-month-old son. "Go ahead and start him on solid food—rice cereal, apple-sauce, and gradually, whatever you eat."

"Salmon?" I asked. "That's what we eat."

She gave me a startled look. "I've never had anyone ask me that," she said. Ah, yes . . . she was from the Midwest. "I suppose if you mash it up and make sure there are no bones, it would be okay. It's all protein. Yes," she said, talking herself into the idea. "That would probably be fine."

Well, I thought, it better be fine, because that's what he's getting. Welcome to Alaska, Doc.

And it was fine. That was the child who had to be chased away from the salmon drying racks as a toddler, unless we wanted sticky fingerprints on all the best pieces of sweet, soft-smoked fish. I have photos of him gleefully dancing in the sunshine by our little smokehouse, waiting for a treat the way other kids wait for candy.

It's an inherited trait. The maternal line of his family has scales.

By western standards, we are longtime Alaskans. We've been here four generations—five, if you count our sailors and steamboat men who brought gold-seekers north from Seattle in the 1890s. It's nothing compared to friends whose families go back eight or nine thousand years here, but it's a start. I don't think we're going anywhere.

We have always been a water people. In the early 1800s, the Gores left the west coast of Ireland for the Great Lakes of North America, where they bought a small schooner. The next generation ran steamboats on the Columbia River, and the next moved up the Pacific Coast to Alaska, to Juneau and Ketchikan. Always west, always north, as if rain and fog could blur the indignity of having their Irish land seized by the English courts, starting the whole migration. And more often than not, they worked on the water, by sail and steam, coal and diesel, or worked with people who did.

The cool temperatures, moist air, and "water, water everywhere" raised up generations of girls with good skin and shiny hair. Girls in bandannas and jeans, often working on the slime line or the salmon tenders or the crab boats with their brothers and cousins; kids who grew up eating smoked salmon instead of bacon with their pancakes. When war came, the boys joined the merchant marine or the navy. Care packages from home perfumed barracks and dorms and offices with the familiar, comforting aroma of canned fish.

One of my favorite cookbooks is my grandmother's battered, coverless copy of the 1929 *Choice Recipes by Ketchikan Women*. In those days, and in that island town, a "salad" meant something with gelatin, or canned fruit, or gelatin and canned fruit. Lettuce is mentioned only as a garnish. There's a section on how to coax children to drink canned milk. And the very first chapter—even before the appetizers—is for fish. Salmon on toast, salmon balls, scalloped salmon with potatoes. Salmon patties, salmon chop, salmon loaf. Salmon canned, pickled, smoked, fried, and roasted. Sautéed salmon roe, salmon in puff pastry with hollandaise sauce, even salmon baked with bananas. In a Catholic household, at a time when Fridays required fish for dinner, that little cookbook got a good workout.

Mom never tasted tuna fish until she left home for college; her father wouldn't have it in the house. Salmon fueled Ketchikan, it paid his salary, and that's what his family ate.

Here's a family secret: They were on what has long been considered the "wrong side" of the fish trap issue. Most traps were owned by large corporations based outside the territory and were so efficient at harvesting salmon that independent fishermen couldn't compete. In 1956, when Alaskans approved a proposed constitution, they also voted overwhelmingly to ban fish traps, a move that went into effect with statehood. But before that happened, Grandpa Gore, who financed law school by working as a second mate in the merchant marine, owned a fish trap himself. He and his law partner helped bring the first Pinkerton men to Alaska to crack down on fish pirates.

In the 1940s, his sons worked their way through college as watchmen on floating fish traps. It sounds romantic—a summer on the ocean, surrounded by spectacular mountains plunging into turbulent seas, bounteous fresh air and wildlife everywhere. Except for the part about living in a tiny, one-room shack in the rainiest part of Alaska with a cantankerous old-timer. There was no radio or television, no neighbors. There were regular visits from the cannery boats coming to collect salmon from the trap and irregular visits from night buyers—the fish pirates eager to pilfer a share of the salmon corralled in the trap. Otherwise, the two oddly matched partners, greenhorn and experienced hand, would read, cook, and try to keep seasickness at bay and sanity within reach. They kept the nets clear of kelp and debris, and took an occasional potshot at raiding sea lions. My uncles came home at the end of summer with their clothes stiff with saltwater and sweat, eager for news, music, movies, and who knows what.

Now, more than sixty years later, our large extended family works those same waters. While their buddies look for summer internships in the city, our children follow the family DNA to the sea. My sons and nephews (and an occasional niece) take turns working on two family-owned fish tenders, vessels that trundle back and forth between processing plants and the fishing grounds. Fishermen want to fish, not waste time running back and forth to town, so the tenders are their lifeline. The tenders bring fresh water, ice, groceries, replacement parts, new crew members. A good tender will offer tired fishing crews hot coffee and homemade cookies or cake. Then their huge vacuum hoses suck salmon out of the fishing boat holds, transfer them into tanks of ice water, and bring them to the plant.

Today's tenders sail with radar, satellite navigation, and more electronics than a video arcade. There are hot showers and computer access. There are movies, stacks of paperbacks, and quick visits to town every few days. If cantankerous old-timers become an issue, a guy can go down to the engine room and scream curses into the diesel engine's roar, and no one will know.

Back at home, my sisters, cousins, and I keep an eye on our kids from long distance. We have the National Marine Weather Service bookmarked on our computers and on speed dial. When the weather kicks up or a boat goes down, we watch the news and send up prayers.

When dark fears shimmer deep, we focus on surface thoughts. We teach our new-to-Alaska neighbors how to home-process fish, turning a packing line into a party with cold beer and the hum of vacuum sealers. Now, all our friends have learned to save their salmon bellies, savoring the richest meat like the bears do.

On weekends, our Little Chief smokers perfume suburban neighborhoods—would that even be allowed in some upscale subdivision Outside? No potluck is complete without at least two varieties of salmon spread; no summer barbecue is official without salmon on the grill; no visit from Dad feels right without a sampler of pickled fish. Around campfires and canning jars, we discuss the option of dropping a few sliced jalapenos into a jar of fish, and question the wisdom of rinsing salmon after brining. Those who refuse to participate in this philosophical conversation, who say they "really don't like fish," are regarded with pity or suspicion; they have clearly never had salmon cooked right—in other words, the way we do it.

In September we sigh with relief and welcome the tender gang home again. They toss their fish-slime-permeated clothes into the trash and stuff the freezer with seafood. They lay plans to head out for the next run, or perhaps go crabbing or back to college. When they were little, the funky odors of low tide would bring their parents' pronouncement, "That's the smell of money." Now, that money is their own down payment on a house, on a car, on schooling.

These are kids who grew up in Seattle, Ketchikan, Kodiak, Dutch Harbor. They went on elementary school field trips to fish hatcheries and had spelling words like "alevin" and "smolt." They grew up eating salmon burgers in the school cafeteria and spotting for hungry seals approaching the family net. As youngsters, they'd roll their eyes when following their grandpa up and down the docks critiquing boats, but now they do it on their own. They listen to the talk on the radio and on the docks and in the bars and in the wheelhouse about fish openings and closures, about predictions for next year, about low runs and overflowing nets, about what makes a good skipper and a safe ship and a profitable season.

Each year they learn a little more. Now, my generation has realized that the next generation is making its own plans for running the business. They want to do it their way. These kids have grown up with the business, and they all want to help, if only part-time or in a small way. So this one will run the boats, and that one will keep the books. The artist can design a company logo. The aspiring filmmaker will help with marketing, and the would-be lawyer will learn fish politics. They are reading up on foreign fleets and fish biology and diesel mechanics. They are stepping up.

And then the summer comes again, and the tenders head out to sea with the latest batch of Gore cousins. The salmon flash silver in the water beneath them. They are all descendants. The distant ancestors of these fish fed the great-grandparents of these kids and their grandparents and parents.

The salmon and hard work are their heritage. The gift is not taken for granted. That heritage has fed our families for generations. It has educated us, and it has put clothes on our back, money in the bank, and adventure and freedom in our souls.

The next run of fish comes up the channel, and the next generation is waiting.

I love remembering my great-grandmother and great-grandfather, Anna and Paul Chukan.

Umma, my great-grandmother, would always have good food waiting for us when we would come back from fishing. As we sat down, she would say to us, "Eat full." One of the things she would make that was always profoundly pleasing was her fish soup. The ingredients were basic: good-sized cubes of salmon with their skin still on, a few pieces of spaghetti broken into the pot along with a handful of rice grains, a few rings of onion and a little bit of salt. The broth was as clear as water with drops of fish oil resting on top. It didn't seem like it would taste like much, but the flavor was amazing. The miracle of this soup was on the order of the fabled Stone Soup, but better. Better because we knew that this soup came from the unconditionally loving hands of our Umma and the salmon was from the ever-giving generosity of the Naknek River, our home stream.

When I first started fishing at age ten my great-grandfather was still part of our family operation. One time he and I were left to pick a piece of gear after it had been floated up the beach, and the rest of our crew went on down to pick our other site. We had a lot of fish to get out of the gear, but my young and awkward hands kept working through it as Grandpa and I worked side by side. I was happy to be doing something other than hauling and happy to be with my grandpa. Although he could not see the fish very well with his old eyes, his hands knew how to get through the gear. The longer we picked, the less clumsy my hands felt. As I felt my skill growing, next to me I could feel my grandpa's strength waning and I could not help but have mixed feelings. Those feelings subsided when I sensed his pride. It was as if I could feel him passing a torch of sorts.

Melanie Brown
Juneau

The Way of the Real Human Being: A Way of Life for Alaska Native Peoples

ILARION "LARRY" MERCULIEFF

Ilarion "Larry" Merculieff is an Unangan (Aleut) born and raised in a traditional way on St. Paul Island in the Pribilofs of the Bering Sea. A recognized expert on traditional ways, he is working on his third book, "Tanax Awaa: The Work of the Land."

ONE DAY WHEN I WAS ABOUT FIVE YEARS OLD I went out with my grandfather to pray near the shore of the Bering Sea. It was an incredibly beautiful day: brilliant with sunshine and without wind. As we walked home along the beach, our feet fell into a slow rhythmic pace along the dark-colored sands. Small waves crested in rapid succession. We could hear seagulls calling from nearby as well as seals bellowing from a distant rookery. The sea air smelled fresh, and everything seemed particularly alive and intense. I could see the horizon for 180 degrees.

"Oh, I love this day!" I proclaimed.

"Anaan eestahnaan Laakaiyax," my grandfather said softly. *"Tututhaax."*

Though still very young, I understood what he was saying. He was teaching me how to be a real human being through the age-old ways Unangan (Aleut) people have used to survive and thrive in the Bering Sea. He was telling me that words are unnecessary, that they diminish the fullness of meaningful human experience. He was asking me to stop talking and to experience the world around me without words. *Don't say anything, boy. Listen.*

St. Paul Island, where I was born and raised, is one of five islands known as the Pribilofs, named for the Russian sea captain who, in 1786, overheard Aleut people in the Aleutians tell of fur seal islands and decided to look for them. St. Paul is a magical and mystical place, a windswept outpost of volcanic rock twelve miles long and five miles wide in the middle of the Bering Sea, about eight hundred miles from Anchorage. My people—the Aleut people—have lived on and along the shores of the Bering Sea for ten thousand years, and we live there still. In my childhood, St. Paul was home to some 1.4 million fur seals, 2.5 million seabirds, a thousand reindeer, an untold number of Arctic foxes, and five hundred Aleut people.

Salmon do not reach the Pribilof Islands because the islands have no rivers, and fur seals intercept and eat those that migrate past. Still, many of the experiences I had growing up, much of what I learned, I later found manifested in the Salmon Nation peoples' fish camps. These places along the Yukon, Kuskokwim, and Copper Rivers are where Athabascans and Yupiks go to catch salmon and process them. After my visits we would often exchange salmon for halibut (the great fish of the Bering Sea) or simply send fish to families we knew were struggling. Again, this came from the ethic I was raised with: Share whatever fish or animal we had with our extended families on St. Paul. It was only natural to share with our farther away extended families.

That ethic of sharing is just part of a much larger principle and worldview I grew up with and found again and again among Alaska Native peoples, whether in fish camps or fishing with hand-held lines: We are all connected. The Aleut to the halibut, the Athabascans and Yupiks to the salmon—each to the other, the rivers to the seas, the shores to the foraging foods, the north to the south, east to west, through storms and calm we are *all* fishing for something that keeps us alive. And we are all connected.

That is why I am telling this story of how I grew up and what I have learned along the way. It is not about salmon. Or is it?

I was blessed to have a fully traditional upbringing, by which I mean I was raised by my entire village in the ways of the real human being. I was always welcomed into everyone's home and treated as if I were a member of the family. I was never scolded for anything and had the freedom to roam the island anytime day or night without restriction. Basically, as with most children in that time and place, I was free to explore my world inside and out without interference by adults.

Between the ages of four and six, I lived with Papa (my grandfather, Paul Merculieff), as was the custom at that time. I went to work with him, hunted with him, prayed with him, slept with him. It was a way for my grandfather to get to know me and for me to get to know my grandfather. Of course I was allowed to engage in other traditional activities during this time. The elders would invite me to go camping with them, and I would listen to their stories. The men would take me out hunting and fishing. The women would take me out to gather wild foods and later invite me to be with them while they prepared and cooked the foods. The villagers were my teachers.

I found my aachaa at the age of five. Although there is really not a trans-lation, *aachaa* can apply to a once-in-a-lifetime mentor, spiritual guide, and/or exceptionally wise companion. An aachaa relationship develops between an older person and a child based on energetic and spiritual con-nections rather than family ties. These relationships are not planned; they just happen when, for whatever reason, each feels an inexplicable bond. During the next eight years of my childhood, my aachaa took me under his wing. We hunted Steller sea lions, eider ducks, and whatever other migra-tory ducks came through. We fished for halibut. From him, I learned much of what I know about relationship and reciprocity, the Aleut ethics and values of sharing, my relationship to myself and to the natural world, and what it means to be an Aleut and a man. In all that time, from age five to thirteen, my aachaa spoke no more than about two hundred words to me. He gave no verbal instructions or explanations; he did not encourage me to ask questions. We were together in silence most of the time. He did expect me to watch, listen, and learn on my own, using my inherent intelligence.

This is typical of our people and indeed of all the indigenous cultures in Alaska. Words are not only superfluous, but they may even constrain our intelligence. Adults never presumed any limitation to my intelligence or ability to learn, nor did they try to tell me what I should learn. Instead, they provided learning opportunities. The adult's responsibility was to create a big open space in which the young one can learn through observation, listening, and being present. What I learned depended totally upon my own interests, initiatives, experiences, interpretations, and intelligence. The only times adults intervened were for reasons of safety. In many other cultures, children are taught to give the "right" answers, from material that others have decided is age appropriate. None of the things I learned about being Aleut came from books, and there were no wrong answers, only better or different ones. The Aleut learning process helped me to think creatively and critically, both ways that have helped immensely in my life and career. Understanding that human and other animal intelligence comes not only from the mind but from the body and spirit, we learn to fine-tune *all* our senses: from hearing, smelling, and seeing to our own intuitive "heart" sense. Underneath the physical, I came to understand that I am profoundly connected to All That Is.

As young hunters, we would sit on volcanic basalt boulders next to the sea for six to eight hours at a stretch, waiting for a sea lion to come by. Steller sea lions are central to the Pribilof Aleut way of life, much as salmon are to most cultures in Alaska. While hunting, we learned to be quiet inside and out and to pay attention to everything going on around us. Conversation was a distraction we could not afford. It might prevent us from sensing the sea lion out in the water, five or even ten miles away. I sat in silence with my aachaa and the other hunters for hours. I listened to the rhythm of the winds. I listened to the seals barking along the beach. I breathed deeply in the fresh sea air. The sun might shine through the clouds. Everything around me would be moving and alive. Sometimes, I let the rhythm of the wind and the waves and sounds of seals lull me into a serene stupor. Once in a while I might even doze off, having been up since three in the morning to be at the shore by six for a full day of hunting that typically lasted late into the afternoon. But I noticed that the men never once dozed off or fell into daydreaming. Their awareness never slipped for a second. And then, suddenly, a hunter would proclaim, *"Cowax ukukohx!"* A sea lion is coming! Instantly, without anyone pointing, all the men would look to the same spot out in the open Bering Sea. Uncannily, the hunters would know a sea lion was coming even before anyone could physically see it. This seemed truly magical.

It is impossible to put into words an experience that goes beyond words; such are the limits of language. As my awareness deepened, I, too, learned to stay fully alert out on the rocks, to feel the sea lion before I could see it. More consistently, I could feel a halibut before it hit my jig fishing line. I could tell how the fish was hooked (by the lip, jaw, or torso). I could determine size and weight. Frequently, I would be able to tell if it was male or female. That kind of inner knowing is inexplicable by empirical standards, but it is nevertheless quite real. It is a mark of manhood to me and my people, and for all cultures of Alaska.

When I had the privilege of going to Athabascan and Yupik salmon fish camps several times in my life, I found that the basis of learning in my childhood was the same for these cultures. Today, fishing for salmon continues to be the mainstay of the different cultures. Athabascan and Yupik peoples, for example, continue to travel yearly to their fish camps to catch, dry, and store the fish that will sustain them through the winter. The people who fish today can trace their fishing roots in these communities back hundreds of generations and know that the salmon are life giving.

What is left unsaid is what salmon really means to the peoples of Alaska. Catching salmon is done by families and extended families, playing an important role in bonding the families together, similar to experiences in my childhood where we did things as groups and extended families. The girls learn the task of cutting up salmon, smoking or drying them, and the ethics and values related to working together with their peers and the adults. The boys watch, listen, and learn how to catch salmon. Both boys and girls learn about sharing, cooperation, and traditional ways of being from the adults. The men and women in turn bond with the children, take salmon in the traditional ways, and teach the young through their actions and demeanor. Stories are told in the evenings after the day is done, providing entertainment and another source of teaching the young. The value of working as a unit rather than as individuals is emphasized. Earth-based pace is the standard all follow, knowing that one must be present in the moment, paying attention to what one is doing in order to do the task well and to be safe. This requires paying attention to what the river, the weather, and one another are doing at all times. Much of what is learned or taken in is visual, nonverbal information. To talk a lot or to ask a lot of questions may distract the individuals from the work at hand or result in taking actions that are not safe, jeopardizing themselves and others.

There are periods of extended silence in fish camp, much like when I went out hunting or fishing with St. Paul adults. Teaching the value of silence is something practiced every day in myriad forms by the adults and elders. Silence teaches one to listen without interruption when someone is speaking. It teaches how to listen without agenda, where the agenda is to prepare a response while the person is still speaking. Listening without agenda causes one to truly consider what another is saying. And pauses before speaking leave time for full consideration of what another is saying.

In going to fish camp, the young man or woman learns, through observation, about the river and her moods, how to look out for obstacles, about the weather and the types of vegetation that are around the camp, how to spot irregularities in individual fish (in terms of texture, taste, color, and smell), what animals are around the camp, where to find berries near the camp, where to go to find fish, how to navigate the river safely. This is place-based learning. What is learned is remembered for the rest of the young people's lives, and it is applied to other places where they may go near their communities.

At fish camp, the young learn about respecting diversity by what they are exposed to by the adults and elders. Appreciation of diversity of thought and learning styles is modeled by the actions and demeanor of the adults and elders as they demonstrate patience, true listening, and making room for different learning styles of the young. Learning about how species relate to each other was an important lesson for me. It is something I have carried in my life and my activism. I learned about the connections of all things in the environment. When salmon are picked up by eagles, bears, and other creatures and carried away to be eaten, their remains decompose and are used by the trees, tundra grasses, and soil, thus contributing to the health of the vegetation.

It was also through traditional activities that I learned what the young people of other cultures learn, about relationship to self, to others, and to the natural world. These lessons are carried deep into the community and the lands on which they depend. According to the elders, relationship is what life is all about. With proper relationship to self, it is easier to have proper relationships with others, with family members, with the community, with fish and wildlife, and with the Earth. Elders say that nothing is created outside until it is created or experienced inside. In other words, what we do outside through our actions is a reflection of what we do inside to ourselves. We trash the environment outside because we are trashing our own internal environment. We create conflict outside because we are in conflict inside. We criticize and judge others because we are critical and judgmental of our selves inside.

The salmon fish camps, hunting, gathering, and other ways of fishing are powerful connections that keep our indigenous cultures intact. However, the health and numbers of salmon and other species are threatened by ever-more-efficient factory trawlers, local and global climate changes, increasing sportfishing and hunting, and on-going industrial development. Additionally, laws, regulations, and western research and management pose unique problems for Alaska Native peoples who must now navigate through a growing host of rules and regulations to take salmon and other species from their own traditional subsistence grounds. And finally, there needs to be a broad redefinition by policymakers of Alaska Native ways of knowing. The vital, real-time, year-round information that comes from these ways of knowing is still marginalized in our society and considered anecdotal by those who make the decisions. This is because fish, wildlife, and habitat research and management must follow the laws and policies that state that they must use the "best available science" in making those decisions. By definition, "best available science" excludes Native ways of knowing.

Alaska Native peoples are ready for substantive partnerships with those agencies making resource and management decisions. Still, they need the playing field to be leveled. And they need allies to support their efforts to protect the fish, wildlife, and habitat that define and sustain the cultures of Alaska. At a time when Earth's life support systems are being pushed to the edge, we need other ways of knowing to complement and supplement western science and management regimes.

Humpy Heads:
Onions, carrots, and
Eyes afloat in fishy broth
Soup that sees you back

> *Thomasina Andersen*
> *Cordova*

Teaching my children
Cutting salmon mom taught me
Hold ulu tight, cut soft

> *Maija Lukin*
> *Kotzebue*

Sunny summer day
Clean and combed, sitting in church
Scales flash from my arm

> *Barbara Njaa*
> *Nikiski*

I Am Now the Age She Was

DAN O'NEILL

Dan O'Neill, of Fairbanks, was born and raised in San Francisco and moved to Alaska in 1975. He is the author of three books: *The Firecracker Boys, The Last Giant of Beringia,* and *A Land Gone Lonesome.*

I HAVE FISHED ON COMMERCIAL GILLNETTERS a few times as a totally green deckhand, on the boats of pals who let me come along when I begged. God, I love it. Mostly just the being there. Whenever I rhapsodize about it, and people seem puzzled, my wife explains, "For him it is mostly about eating." That is true. The high life for me is frying up a fresh sea-run Dolly or whatever gift comes aboard: garlic, butter, onions, the smell of it, a bottle of white wine pulled from a cool spot in the hold, the breezes streaming through open windows, the boat rolling, the volcanoes rolling too, into view, out of view, changing places with the flashing blue water.

And it is a fine thing to sleep at anchor, in a narrow bunk, rocked by the sea. To roll into unconsciousness with one idée fixe: breakfast. Fish and coffee, grits and butter. The captain's stories. A snowy volcano practically pulled up to the table.

I know. The net of my memory does not catch the work.

My grandpa had a shack near Fetters in Sonoma County, and we'd go "up the country" every summer. My brother and I were quite small when my father started taking us to a little creek near Boyes Springs, to a pool where he swam as a child. The smell of the willows, oaks, and bays, the smell of the mud, and of that part of the creek that flows through the air, all have embedded themselves in my memory. I can smell too the wetted bread he taught us to wad up to bait the tiny hooks to catch fingerling trout. Part of what I love about fishing is how amazingly much there is in common between that childhood tableau and every other kind of fishing I've ever done, no matter the scale.

The summer I was nine—I date it by the songs on the radio—we started fishing for juvenile striped bass on the Napa River, or a slough of it. My father would wake me in the dark before dawn to make the drive down through the Valley of the Moon and then east over the hills into Napa County. "I get the radio going; you get it coming," he'd say. Somehow, my city-born old man had latched on to country music, so, going, it was KSAY's Big Country Corral and songs of busted love or of some guy's momma. Coming home, I'd flip between the teenager stations. The owner of a bait shop said we could fish from a derelict whaleboat tied up to the bank. It had high gunwales that made it a safe spot for me and later my little brother. My father would cut some bait and stab his mother-of-pearl-handled knife into the plank seat. "Nickel to the first fish," he'd say.

I think my strong connection to nature and the outdoors formed while fishing, and, crazily enough, mostly within the city limits of San Francisco. I can hear my father's voice rasp from the dark in the *r*-dropping San Francisco accent you used to hear: "Put on two undershirts and two pairs of pants." While I hunted up my clothes, he'd push the car out of the garage. Not to wake the others, he'd start it in the driveway. I'd get the long surf rods from off the wall in the garage and thread them through the rear window of the Ford. I could see the fog rolling by the streetlight on the corner, as the cold robbed the last trace of heat I carried from my bed.

We didn't have any good warm clothes. No long johns, no knit caps, no boots, no gloves of any kind. Though—or maybe because—not so many years earlier, he'd spent the bitter winter of 1944–45 in the Ardennes and marching into the Rhineland, my father didn't feel we needed to buy any special gear. "You could stuff some newspaper under your jacket," he might say.

Fosters cafeteria on Twenty-First and Geary was open early, and we'd have scrambled eggs and bacon, a raisin snail and coffee. He'd buy a *Chronicle* and shake out the Sporting Green for me. I'd see how the Giants were doing.

We liked to go down to the end of Baker's Beach, the end near the bridge. We were surf casters. Bait fishermen. We'd trudge all the way down there with poles and sand spikes, him with the rucksack, me with a box of frozen sardines or anchovies covered with rock salt, wrapped in newspaper, tied up with twine.

I'd wait for a big wave, chase it out until it gathered and sprang, and then cast, turn, and run quickly with the pole over my shoulder. It was good to hold the rod a while, listening with my hands, filtering out the throbs and jerks that were nothing but waves and undertow. After a while, I'd plant the pole in the sand spike and put my hands in my pockets. Stand and wait for fish. Wait for the sun to clear the Oakland hills, climb down the orange bridge, and finally warm me. Down the line a ways, my father faced the ocean with his hands on his hips. He looked like a tough man squared up to an imponderable.

Stripers were what we prized the most, but I was happy with a shark, or a big flounder. Just so it fought hard and was work to land. Sometimes we caught the slim-bodied horse smelt, or some fat little perch, or sand dabs. But shark or bass or sand dab, we took whatever we caught to my grandmother out in the Mission District. Many years later, I would see the place where she grew up: the ruins of a stone cottage with a dirt floor. The gable ends with their chimneys standing in a shaggy, wind-tossed field, yards from Galway Bay. My grandmother was happy with any kind of fish we brought. She made soup with the heads.

I am now the age she was then. And I think fish mean to me now more of what they meant to her then when she took out her knives and, probably, thought of home.

But for me, not just the possessing but the catching of fish feeds something. For almost thirty years I fished for king salmon in a certain river in central Alaska with a pal I'd known from San Francisco days. He'd found the spot. The way in was a long, swampy, bug-ridden, deadfall-strewn, bushwhacking, game trail proposition that took the better part of two hours to walk. On top of that, we had to cross land possessed by parties hostile to our entry: an absentee Indian tribe and resident grizzly bears.

Jonnie showed me how to tie yarn flies and to rig for bouncing them along the bottom. He also imparted his ethics. We didn't use high-test line or landing nets or chest waders. We ran with those big fish wherever they went, gaining what we could, when we could, for maybe three-quarters of an hour, until, both man and fish exhausted, the noble beast might let go without a lot of indignity.

Jonnie had other, quasi-religious proscriptions that I did not observe. He grew up in the foothills of the Sierras in California where his father taught him to fish the trout streams. One time, the teenaged Jonnie managed to hook and land a very large and beautiful trout. The big daddy of the stream. When his father saw it, he said, "Are you going to keep it?" Jonnie hadn't for an instant considered releasing the fish. Probably, he was already imagining how he'd show it off to his mother and siblings. The idea made him think for a moment, though. But only for a moment, and he killed that fish. Still, this strange question from his father was a seed. And when it had rooted sufficiently—some time after his father's premature death—it became a tenet. During all the years I fished with him, no matter the circumstance, he threw the first king back. A propitiation of the fish gods, I'd say, glibly. But I knew it as an act of expiation.

My father died way too young too. Then Jonnie died at fifty-seven. I took a scoop of his ashes to that place we'd go. Now, our river's kings are dying too. Fireweed and roses grow up in the abandoned fish camps along the Yukon River. Soon smokehouse poles will poke through as ruins. For now, my nieces and nephews bring me a few stunted kings from their family's waning fish camp. I'm happy to get them. I make soup with the heads.

One cold and rainy fall afternoon I stood on the rocky beach at Seward to try to catch a silver salmon. There were two other people on the beach, two men fishing close to each other. I walked a good distance down from them, cast out, and pulled in a fish. Not being an experienced fish catcher at the time, I yelled down to the guys: "Hey, is this one a keeper?" They looked at me and then silently turned back to their fishing. I took the fish off the hook and put it back in the water. One more cast, one more salmon. I called out to them again: "Hey, how about this one?" Still no response, but it was bigger than the last one and looked pretty nice, so I laid it out on the beach. On my third cast, I caught one more. This time I walked toward them a bit before yelling the same thing. This time one finally responded: "You caught it, lady. You decide!" I packed up and carried my two nice silvers back up the beach. As I passed them, one said: "We've been out here in the rain all morning without a single bite. Then here you come, and every time you throw your line in, you catch a fish." That's all they said.

Karen Maskarinec
Chugiak

As a child growing up harvesting salmon and various other fish, you enjoy it a lot. As you grow you realize it's not just about catching fish but about the people you do it with, the early morning coffee and conversation, the stories, the laughs, and the travels and sights you see. You do all this while connecting with nature and with a smile on your face, rain or shine.

George Gatter
Kodiak

The King and I

RICHARD CHIAPPONE

Rich Chiappone is the author of two story collections. His fiction and nonfiction have appeared in national magazines, including *Alaska Magazine, Gray's Sporting Journal,* the *Missouri Review, Playboy,* and the *Sun.* He lives in Homer and teaches at the Kachemak Bay Campus of Kenai Peninsula College and in the MFA program at the University of Alaska Anchorage.

IN 1653 IZAAC WALTON, one of the earliest commentators on the world of fishing, called salmon the "king of fish" in his famous tome, *The Compleat Angler.* Almost exactly three hundred years later, I sat on the living room floor of my best friend Danny Humic's house in the industrial Rust Belt city of Niagara Falls, New York, watching what had to be one of the earliest TV fishing shows. On the screen, Lee Wulff, angling guru and raconteur, stood grinning at the camera somewhere in remote Quebec or Labrador, holding up an Atlantic salmon as long as my nine-year-old leg. The fish looked like a chrome-plated torpedo with eyes.

Yes, the fish was fabulous, but I certainly didn't think of it as kingly. At that age the allure of royalty was beyond me: I was more interested in King Kong than King Arthur. What impressed me most was the absence of houses, telephone poles, and, most important, factories along that heavenly wild Canadian river. I lived one block inland from the Niagara River and a few blocks upstream from the big plants lining its shore: Hooker Chemical,

DuPont, Union Carbide, International Graphite. Day and night, they spewed black soot and sulfurous fumes into the air, and God knows what into the river. The nearest Atlantic salmon streams were hundreds of miles to the east, the nearest Pacific salmon, thousands of miles west.

Although my father had little interest in the sport, I became a fisherman for some reason. One block to the north of our street, the boys my age played whiffle ball, joined Little League, became high school jocks; one block to the south, the boys leaned into the engines of their fathers' cars and counted the days to their learner's permits. On our street, boys fished. All of which would have been positively idyllic, except that a good day of fishing on the pollution-ravaged Niagara was one with a couple stunted perch in it, a bullhead, maybe a carp.

One morning, on our walk to school, a friend and fishing buddy named Bob Hawkins announced that his family was moving to Vancouver, British Columbia. He produced what must have been a field guide to western fishes, and we studied the drawings of the five Pacific salmon species he'd soon be hauling in. The beautiful green-headed, red-bodied, spawning sockeye fascinated me. Oh, Bob Hawkins would definitely catch some of those—the lucky bastard. British Columbia, on the distant opposite edge of the continent, was clearly a province in the Kingdom of the Salmon. It never occurred to me that Vancouver was a real city, much larger than my own town, and that there would be all kinds of buildings there too—perhaps even factories. Salmon lived there, or near there. That was all I needed to know. Longing for the day I would catch, or even simply see, a live salmon, I focused on the next best thing, and the only alternative within reach: the King of Fish's vassal, the trout.

When we were in fifth grade, Danny Humic's father took Danny and me to a children's fishing derby at a manmade pond somewhere south of Buffalo. There might have been a hundred of us kids encircling that little pond in the dawn mist when the sheriff fired the starting shot. A hundred spinning lures and baited hooks sailed out—many crisscrossing, of course. My first trout, a hatchery-raised brown, maybe ten inches long, came in fifteenth place. For days afterward, I kept it in the refrigerator and proudly showed it to anyone I could corner. I wouldn't let my mother cook it. At the end of the week, sick of the odor, she apologetically tossed it in the trash.

For the next ten years, trout would be the closest thing to salmon I would see. Yes, they are lovely little fish, among the most beautiful in the world, as Izaac Walton and every other fishing writer since has declared many times over, but they lack the grandeur, the sovereign status of their liege lords. And the hatchery-stocked waters that trout inhabited—at least those within range of my weekend fishing trips with Danny and his father—were not the grandly wild salmon rivers of my dreams. Not even close.

Now, if I'd been more adventurous, I might have traveled straight to salmon country after graduating from high school and college. Another friend, Jerry Presti, did just that. Some time before the Marine Mammal Protection Act of 1972, Jerry loaded his fishing rods and hunting rifles into a VW bus and drove four thousand miles from Niagara Falls to Alaska. He shot a moose and—for some reason I can't even fathom today—a harbor seal the size of Danny Humic's TV console. He had the dead pinniped stuffed and displayed it in the very small living room of the Presti house on Sixty-Eighth Street.

Nearly forty-five years later, what I remember most about Jerry's Alaskan adventure was the 8mm home movie of him catching wild silver salmon in a misty rain forest river, far from the factories of our town. Yes, I wanted so badly to do that too, but instead I dropped out of school and married very young, and the Kingdom of the Salmon remained unreachable for a long, long while. With no education and a wife and daughters to support, I painted houses and commercial buildings and even the chemical tanks of the big factories I'd grown up alongside. I spent my twenties climbing steel towers and pipe racks overlooking the Niagara, trying, in a way, to see the wild rivers over the horizon.

And then the mountain came to Mohammed. Sort of. By the late 1960s, native game fish in the Great Lakes (muskie, bass, walleye, and lake trout) were nearly extirpated by overfishing, pollution, habitat destruction, and predation by nonindigenous sea lampreys. With the large, top-of-the-food-chain fish depleted, the population of another invasive species, herring-like alewives, exploded so rapidly the lakes couldn't support them; they died off each year by the millions, their rotting carcasses fouling beaches. In 1966 the state of Michigan began stocking Pacific coho (silver) salmon in Lake Michigan to prey on the alewives. The program proved so successful, and the big game fish so popular with sportsmen, New York State followed suit, planting coho and chinook (king) salmon in Lake Ontario and Lake Erie tributary streams.

Suddenly I had salmon in my own backyard. Problem solved. Dreams attained.

Well, not exactly.

To begin with, the newly introduced salmon could not reproduce in most local creeks, where warm summer water temperatures and shallow gradients prevented the oxygenation needed for viable eggs. That meant it was a put-and-take, hatchery-dependent fishery. And the sluggish streams—formerly habitat mostly for sunfish and suckers—didn't exactly meet my Kingdom of the Salmon expectations either, no matter how many lordly fish the state dumped in. An additional pall was cast over the whole enterprise by the official warnings that salmon from Lake Erie and Lake Ontario streams could contain PCBs, dioxin, mirex, and other potential carcinogens. My hometown, Niagara Falls, is also the home of Love Canal, one of the country's first Superfund toxic waste cleanup sites. All in all, it was a rather incongruous and dystopian realm for the King of Fish. Picture the British royals relocating to a coal town in Wales.

Still, salmon, right under my nose. The pragmatic thing to do was fish for them.

Sometime in the early 1970s, I caught my first salmon, a fifteen-pound chinook, in the Niagara River gorge, just downstream from the huge Niagara Mohawk Power Company turbine house and directly across the river from the infamously filthy Cyanamid plant on the Canadian shore. It was late in the fall, and the hook-jawed male fish was intent on finding a mate before dying, blissfully unaware of the futility of that whole enterprise. But, unlike salmon pictured in books, this one had not turned an exotic red and green; its whole body was a sickly black. I was unsure how tasty a deteriorating salmon from the less-than-pristine Niagara might be. But, unwilling to just throw it away after dreaming about this moment since I was a child, I brined and smoked that fish—probably adding more carcinogens to those already in it. My mother, always a good sport, served it as an appetizer with Thanksgiving dinner that year. Nobody died. At least not right away.

Over the next decade, I caught salmon from Lake Ontario, Lake Erie, and Lake Huron streams. In a way, I was thankful that they were all darkening spawners; it was easier to simply declare a fish too far gone to eat than try to figure out how toxic it might be. As much as I longed to adore them, the non-native salmon—planted in the Great Lakes to solve a trash fish problem—would always seem misplaced royalty, and unhealthy to boot. And that was my worshipful-fearful relationship with the King of Fish for all of the 1970s.

By 1979 the transplanted Pacific salmon were thriving in the Great Lakes, but my first marriage was foundering. So was the economy of western New York. Divorced and in need of steady employment, I transferred my membership in the International Brotherhood of Painters and Allied Trades to the local union in Las Vegas, Nevada, America's perennial boomtown. There, I found plenty of work as a paperhanger in the endless casino expansions of that time. But a move to the Great American Desert did not get me any closer to wild salmon. Three years in the bleak alkali wastelands of southern Nevada left me aching more than ever for the great northern woods and rivers of my childhood dreams. In 1982 I moved my union book to Anchorage, Alaska, another boomtown—but, this time, one built smack in the middle of the Kingdom of the Salmon.

I caught my first wild, native salmon that spring, a king about the size of the one I had caught ten years earlier in the Niagara gorge. This one, taken from the beautiful little Ninilchik River, a mile upstream from the saltwater of Cook Inlet, was every bit as silvery bright as Lee Wulff's Atlantic salmon had looked on Danny's TV, thirty years prior. It came out of the lovely little stream, twisting and thrashing in the spring sun like the magnificent game fish it was. And this fish had probably never seen a PCB or dioxin molecule in its life.

I have been fishing for kings and every other species of Pacific salmon ever since. I've caught chum salmon on the remote Yukon-Kuskokwim Delta, huge silver salmon on Kodiak Island, and diminutive humpies in the Aleutians. Over the years, I've caught hundreds of sockeye on the world-famous Kenai River—not the strange green-headed creatures of Bob Hawkins's field guide, but chrome-bright fish fresh from the sea, one of the greatest food fish in the world.

In the late 1980s, driven by my desire to fish, and my second wife's love of the boreal forests of the Kenai Peninsula, we bought three acres of dense white spruce forest along the Anchor River, two hundred miles south of Anchorage. There, we quite literally built a life around salmon fishing, starting with a tent platform, where my wife canned our fresh-caught sockeyes on a Coleman stove, and finishing with a two-story home with a cook's kitchen and a spare bedroom for fly-fishing guests. In 2002 when my wife got a job at the high school in the nearby town of Homer, we moved to the Anchor River.

Though the house is about the same distance from the Anchor as the one I grew up in was from the Niagara, the nearest thing to a factory might be one of the salmon canneries in the town of Kenai, about fifty miles to the north. It's an idyllic setting, a little piece of the Kingdom of the Salmon as

I always envisioned it. But after thirty-two years of fishing for salmon, I've noticed lately that I spend more time than I used to thinking about the last chapter of their life cycles, the high-speed senescence that overtakes them when they enter fresh water. Maybe it was receiving my first Social Security check in the mail in September, just when the Anchor River gravel bars and riverbanks were littered with decomposing salmon carcasses and the last of the late spawners writhed and gasped in the shallows around my hip boots, their flesh sliding off, their heads covered in white fungus.

Not to get too morbid, but in a sure sign that the next kingdom I'll be entering is my own dotage, I even wrote a poem about it.

Well, a limerick, actually.

Spawners
The salmon, most noble of trout,
mates, rotting from tail to snout.
With fungus-blind eyes,
it has sex once and dies.
I think I'd as soon go without.

My impertinence notwithstanding, I love the King of Fish and the places where they live. I love to catch them, and I love to cook and eat them. Let's face it: for a working-class kid from Love Canal, they are as close to royalty as I'm ever going to get. Long live the King.

In 2006 when we started setnetting in Uyak Bay on Kodiak Island, there was quite a span between our knowledge and the site's potential. That became apparent when we showed up with a skiff that didn't look like any other skiff in the bay. We didn't know that it mattered whether we used a bow roller or a side roller. We didn't know to add trailer buoys on our anchors. We didn't know that the cannery had a stockroom where we could buy supplies!

Luckily, it turned out that Uyak Bay was full of experienced setnetters who were more than willing to share what they knew. And for the first few years of our Kodiak adventure, we did more waiting to fish than actual fishing. It turns out that was a good thing for us new guys. Our early years included more cabin work than fishing—replacing roofs, digging a well, using gravity and siphons to get water to our cabin, digging an outhouse hole, and replacing pilings. I had never dug a hole before becoming a setnetter. It turns out that digging a hole is the key to independence.

People worry today about how disconnected from nature kids are. This is not the case living as a setnetter. Our family is part of Mother Nature—living in a tidal zone; depending on the ocean's bounty of fish; observing the weather and how it affects our fish, our travels, our recreation, and our safety. Our actions revolve around the tides. We see tides and currents doing their thing all day long and watch how they affect our beach, our fishing operation, our boat. We highlight the negative tides in our tide book so we can search for our favorite invertebrates. We now know a brittle star from a blood star and can easily spot an opalescent nudibranch within moments of flipping a rock. A rock full of barnacles is more alive than I ever knew. I learned all of this at forty; think how cool it will be for my sons when they later realize these are things they have known all their lives.

Our boys are now full-on ocean guys, true assets to our fishing operation who get paid crew shares for the valuable help they provide. How lucky they are to have such comfort and experience on the water. While they still have a lot to learn, the decision making involved with skippering a skiff has given them a perspective on life that is unmatched for most teenagers. They've learned many skills, taken pride in their work, and have learned how to just be—sometimes to do nothing. Our hope is that they look back on these summers and realize the gift of fish camp. While it's about the fish, it's not really about the fish. Life at fish camp is like one of those Mastercard ads that ends with the word *priceless*.

Laurie Bassett
Anchorage

Thank You. Swimmer
EMMA TEAL LAUKITIS

Emma Teal Laukitis was raised on a homestead near False Pass, Alaska. She lives in Homer during winters and continues to fish with her family each summer. Emma graduated from Williams College and now operates a small business, Salmon Sisters, with her sister, Claire.

BEFORE I WAS BORN my mom and dad bought a homestead on the Aleutian Islands. The place was remote—across the bay from a small Aleut village—but alone on the tundra and surrounded by sea. This place, Stonewall Place, and its proximity to fishing grounds seemed a siren's call to my young parents on their first married adventure. Salmon were swimming through the pass and into fishermen's nets. My parents set out to catch their first fish.

With the influx of money from their first salmon seasons, raising children became feasible. My sister was born before the first Area M salmon opener in 1990, and I joined her a year later.

Stonewall Place taught us about survival. Survival was possible with subsistence and self-sustainability. The four of us depended on water to power our waterwheel, driftwood for warmth, and the ocean for food. Our home was isolated, our family insular. We grew strong as an entity—by enduring together and fishing together.

I learned very young that salmon were to be respected. My mom taught my sister and me to weave mats out of long beach grass. These mats became beds for two sides of a salmon, filleted with a beach-found mussel shell. We honored the first fish we caught each summer with a prayer and eagle down in our dandelion-blonde hair. We treat the salmon with respect, my dad taught us, so that when we send the salmon's remains back to the sea, she tells the others to swim to our nets.

The smell of salmon became our own. When we skiffed across the pass to the village for groceries and mail, the postmistress sniffed at us from across the counter. My mom set down a bag of her smoked salmon, the source of our smell, on a book of stamps. The villagers loved Mom's smoked strips. They called it Aleut candy.

Salmon fishing was my first paying job and early source of entertainment. Too young to be of real use, my sister and I were put to work sliming with butter knives the king salmon my dad brought home for my mom's smokehouse. While she filleted and brined the fish, we dissected and tasted and squealed. Not many years later, we were Grundens-clad crew on the back deck of my dad's boat, the *Lucky Dove*.

My family moved to Homer for the winters when my sister and I were old enough to require real schooling. We were timid and uncertain away from the wild Aleutians. But there was already a common language forming between us and a freckled girl from a fish camp in Ugashik, a brother and sister from an Area M drifter, the spirited daughter of a Dillingham setnetting family. Together we were children of a seasonal tradition, returning with our families each summer in search of salmon, the fish that sustained us and defined our collective lives.

I saved my crew share through high school. My mom helped me open a bank account, and my dad emphasized the importance of financial independence. They encouraged my sister and me to put the money we saved toward college tuition.

I thought I didn't have a chance at college. My family didn't come from prestige. I had gaps in my education from homeschooling for eight years in bush Alaska. I read about different colleges in a hand-me-down catalog and dog-eared pages that looked like they might be a good fit, but I had never been to these places, and I couldn't claim to know what I was looking for. When it came time to write the application essays, though, I realized that I did, at least, have a story. And where did this story come from? From those salmon that my parents came to Alaska in search of, that I return to search for each summer

When I arrived at an East Coast college I found myself a curiosity, and I was proud to be an Alaskan. I felt pride for other Alaskans, who I knew to be hard-working and humble. I developed a new admiration for the life I'd left behind, specifically the culture of fishing that seemed obsolete on this other coast.

It was hard to explain my love for salmon. I was surrounded by people who regarded commercial fishing as an antiquated, borderline, barbaric occupation. "How can you say you love salmon when you kill so many of them?"

I swore that it was a ridiculous question, but I didn't know how to answer it yet. I watched how salmon, the tradition of fishing, and my sense of place gave purpose to my studies. In the art studio I witnessed my hands roll a whole thawed salmon from my freezer in ink and print it onto butcher's paper. I felt the way my writing always turned back to some reference to the sea. I couldn't deny the relief my body felt when I ate a jar of smoked salmon my mom had sent, on the worst day of finals, with a fork in the library. The other jars were saved as incentive for completing the hardest rowing practices and the latest nights loading the boat trailer. Salmon gave strength to my body, contributing to four of my team's consecutive NCAA rowing championships.

I felt an intense urge to defend the smell and taste of real salmon when I found something called salmon in the dining hall. That meal of farmed fish baked in refried beans and coffee grounds lacked the familiar sensations of healing and strength, the immediate transfer of energy from fish to human, to which I was accustomed.

Through college my sister and I returned to the Aleutians in summertime to fish. One slow day on the back deck we dreamed up a business for someday. We'd call ourselves a clever name and we'd create art and clothing and make our love for the ocean and our pride for fishing known. While in Italy studying at an art school, I learned how to screen print and started creating the designs that would turn into this business. Now, in my first year after college, my sister and I are learning to be small-business owners of our company, Salmon Sisters. In the first year of our online sales of organic apparel featuring salmon, rockfish, and fanciful mermaids, we've sent packages to more than a thousand Alaskans in coastal communities from Petersburg to Naknek, from St. Mary's to Nome. Our clothing has found its way to Norway, Italy, Madagascar. We are astonished by how many people love the ocean and its creatures.

The truth is, I'm enchanted with salmon, and with those who fish for them. I especially want to celebrate the number of women I know running their own boats and working on deck. These are the women who inspire me. Their hands are slimy and callused. Their hair hasn't been brushed in weeks. They are passionate about their work.

Salmon have given all Alaskans a common language, a set of values, something to believe in and hope for (at the very least, a strong salmon run). Salmon have kept my family close, physically on forty-eight feet of aluminum but also bonded by a fierce connection to the ocean. Salmon have provided me with an education, have given direction to my work as an artist, have offered me physical strength as an athlete, and have been the single thread woven through my friends and my community. Salmon have given me something to work for, to hope for, and to defend.

How does one thank the source of her existence? In my dad's words, *We catch God and we eat her.* We do that with gratitude. And yet, as we know from the fate of salmon elsewhere in the world, we live in a fragile balance. I wonder if I've exploited my relationship with these fish, despite the gratitude I feel and the respect I offer.

When June comes, I'll be honoring our first fish. My family, in the tradition of Alaskan fishermen, will remain resourceful, humble, and cognizant of our responsibilities. I believe in the salmon with my spirit, my heart, my health. You have provided us, Swimmer, with the tools for a rich and rewarding life.

When I was a child, I counted the days until summer when I would visit my dad and brother on Anton Larsen Island off Kodiak. We ran wild through the woods, shot squirrels, picked buckets of berries, slept under the stars, ate honey butter on pilot bread, and—my very favorite—went fishing. With poles or nets, our days spent fishing were the most prized time I spent with my dad and brother as a family. Without a doubt, my love of those moments shaped my life. I now call Kodiak home year-round and have enjoyed summer jobs fishing salmon from Uganik to Bristol Bay. Although fishing hasn't been my profession or even my passion, I feel glad to know that a lifestyle involving salmon has made me who I am today.

Sarah Harrington
Kodiak

As a fly-fishing guide, father, husband, and Alaskan, I depend on Tongass National Forest salmon for my paycheck, my meals, and countless memories with my friends and family. My wife and I met in Alaska nearly ten years ago, and we are so happy to be raising our three-year-old in an environment rich in salmon. When she was just two, our daughter asked Santa for a fly rod for Christmas. This summer she successfully caught her own meals on many fish camp trips, including her first silver!

Matthew Boline
Auke Bay

Stone Fish, Living Mirrors

HANK LENTFER

Hank Lentfer is the author of *Faith of Cranes: Finding Hope and Family in Alaska.* He lives with his wife, Anya, and daughter, Linnea, on the bank of a small salmon stream flowing through Gustavus, Alaska.

A FISH HITS THE FAR END OF THE NET, thrashing the surface, bobbing the floats. I join my family in a raucous round of whoops and hoots and then ease the bow of the skiff toward the entangled fish.

Bent at the waist, leaning over the gunwale, mother and daughter lift the salmon aboard and free it from the snarled web. It's a large, vibrant sockeye, body tense and firm, scales on its back a shimmering gray, brightening to a glistening silver toward the belly. Its upper jaw has just the hint of the downward hook of a male preparing to spawn.

Although it's an annual event, this first fish of the year, quivering on the bottom of the boat, feels like an improbable, marvelous, unexpected gift to emerge from the sea. It's as if the twelve months that separate each visit to this cove is too great a distance to carry a precise memory of the fish's beauty. Each year we are stunned anew.

Our revelry is interrupted by more thrashing at the net. A half dozen sockeyes have hit low, near the lead line. Just as we free the last fish from the web, another salmon, followed quickly by one more, hit high near the corks. We bend to the work, our back muscles filling with a satisfying ache, the bottom of the boat filling with the blood and scales and bodies of the fish. Within a few hours, we have twenty-five salmon. Enough to pack the smoker twice over with a few extra to share fresh with friends and neighbors back at home.

We pull the net aboard and unsheathe knives to clean the catch. Bellies emptied of guts, bodies washed of blood, each fish gets buried into a tote of shaved ice for the long ride back to town. Quick scrub of the boat and, for this year, fishing is done.

With plenty of daylight remaining, we opt for an exploratory hike up the stream at the head of the cove. Pinched between bedrock walls, the water tumbles over and around boulders with a roar that makes it hard to talk. We skirt the riverbank, following a bear trail through the dim, mossy forest and quickly arrive at the calm expanse of a still lake. In a deep, clear pool joining lake to stream, thirty to forty salmon hold in the easy current.

On the way back to the boat, near the tide line, my daughter notices a pattern carved into the stream-side rock. When I catch up with her, Linnea's running her finger through the shallow groove. "Looks like a fish," she says. And sure enough it does; an oblong body with radiating lines for a tail, a single indentation for an eye. Tuned to the shape, we quickly find several more blunt characters of fish swimming in the rocks. Scattered among the fish are abstract shapes, too; concentric circles widen out like ripples from a tossed rock. "Who made these?" my daughter asks, running her finger 'round one of the circles.

The northern portion of Alaska's panhandle, home to the state's capital and a smattering of smaller towns, had an estimated precontact population of six hundred to eight hundred people. The folks who scraped these shapes into stone would have arrived at the stream mouth in a dugout canoe after several days of paddling. Unlike our one-day, zip-in-catch-fish-and-go-home trip, those early paddlers would have stayed for weeks, repairing the summer shelter, erecting racks to dry fish, gathering wood for the smokehouse fire.

"Come look at this one," my wife says, rubbing her hand over a rough slab of bedrock. We gather around and peer at the odd petroglyph she's found—two squiggly lines cut by a series of straight gouges. Coastal Tlingit often constructed in-stream weirs to channel salmon through a single passage. We guess Anya's discovery to be a depiction of such a weir—the wavy lines representing the banks of the stream with straight lines for the wooden fence.

And who, within the small band of people who built and fed themselves from that weir, engraved those shapes into stone? I imagine the adults busy with the chores of fish. Someone dedicated, all day, to the task of hooking salmon; others filleting, smoking, drying, and storing the catch for the long journey back to the village. Perhaps it was the children, left on their own, who filled the long summer afternoons by wrapping their small hands around the perfect stone and telling stories and giggling as they etched these enduring sketches. I can imagine a young girl at summer's end, canoe loaded, parents waiting, stashing that perfect stone beneath a tree root. I can imagine her delight, the following year, in retrieving that tool and finishing the fish she did not have the time to complete the year before.

Or perhaps, rather than a child's doodles, rock art is a way to announce ownership, to let others know they should keep paddling and find their own stream. Whatever the inspiration, salmon occasionally find their way onto the cliff faces and cave walls that have carried bison and deer and other rock art through the ages. The oldest known rock salmon was created twenty-five thousand years ago in a cave on the banks of what today we call the Vézère River in southwestern France. It's a detailed etching complete with eye, mouth, gill cover, and the slightly hooked snout of a male.

The Atlantic salmon that fed and inspired that Paleolithic artist have been displaced from most European rivers since the height of the Industrial Revolution. But what, if anything, of cultural significance is slipping away with the last of Europe's wild salmon? If people living along the Vézère River are well fed, if the fish stalls are filled with the fillets of farmed fish, why fret about the empty river?

Ecologists speak of diversity being the key to a community's resiliency. The tallgrass prairie of North America, comprised of forty to sixty grass species and more than three hundred additional species of forbs and flowers, was endowed with a deep genetic reservoir honed by drought and blight, flood and fire. Salmon themselves, shaped by advancing ice and menacing teeth, flash floods and shifty rivers, have evolved a wide array of lifestyles to cope with a dynamic world. These lessons of the past, encoded in the complex coils of DNA within seed heads and fish eggs, can be unwrapped in response to the trials of the future.

Modern monocultures, on the other hand, whether salmon farms or cornfields, are untested and vulnerable to the arrival of a single pest or the stress of a prolonged drought. This lesson of resiliency has been adopted by financial planners who advocate for a diversity of investments to weather an uncertain future. If one strategy tanks, there is another option to pick up the slack.

As a kid in Alaska, I played with my buddy on the banks of a small creek that flowed near the house. Each summer, that tiny stream filled with the bodies of huge fish. As boys do, we trapped and harassed those poor creatures, spending weeks constructing stone fences in the frigid waters. When we, through persistence and good luck, succeeded in corralling a salmon in a shallow pool, we proudly hauled our catch home, hugging the slimy, wiggling animal to our chests, covering ourselves with scales and blood and stories. At night, lying in bed, those fish swam through our young minds, splashed through dreams, and coursed, literally, through our veins. After breakfast, I'd call my friend and we'd meet creek side to see what changes the night had brought to the parade of fish.

How fortunate I was as a kid to live near that stream. How fortunate I am as a father to stand on a stream bank with my daughter, tracing our fingers over ancient artwork with scales on our boots, blood on our pants, and a cooler load of salmon stashed in the nearby boat.

Rising tide and a gust of wind off the ocean has me thinking of the long ride home. "Sorry to leave but we gotta get going, kiddo." We leave the stream-side art and clamber back into the skiff. An hour later, we're safely off the open ocean and into the protected channels of inside waters. The sky, crowded with gray clouds in the morning, is now broken by blue holes opening to the tinge of rich evening light.

Reluctant for the day to end, we put ashore at one of our favorite beaches. Anya and Linnea gather wood for a fire while I anchor the boat. Paddling to the beach in our little kayak, I pluck a lap-full of wide kelp fronds. As mother and daughter coax the flames into their high pile of sticks, I wrap one of the day's fish in several layers of kelp. Once the flames have settled into glowing coals, we nestle the wrapped fish into the fire's center and cover it with hot embers.

Twenty minutes later, using sticks for tongs, we delicately lift the mummified fish from the smoke and heat and lay it on the gravel beach. The outer layers of kelp are blackened and crisp while the inner layers remain slick and brown. The fish at the center is steaming and moist. My family kneels in a tight circle around the salmon, foreheads almost touching, to pinch hot flakes of muscles from the sockeye's bones and lift them to our smiling lips.

After dinner we head for home. By the time we turn into the river flowing through the center of town, the late summer sun has torched the sky into layers of orange and pink. Our neighbor Vince catches our lines as we pull up to the dock.

"Fresh sockeye?" I ask.

"Of course, how could I say no?" says Vince.

We lift one of the silvery salmon from its bed of ice and hand it over to our friend. In turn, Vince helps us wrestle the heavy cooler of ice and fish from the boat to the truck. During the two-mile drive to the house we hand out more salmon, flagging down friends on the road, knocking on front doors, lifting the lid of the cooler in the back of the truck to share with everyone we meet the beauty of the sea's gifts.

And this, I believe, is the real story of salmon, the story etched into stone around the world, the story of abundance and renewal. Had we been returning home from the store instead of the boat harbor, had we spent the evening checking items off a shopping list instead of picking hot flesh from steaming bones, had we filled the back of the truck with $1,000 worth of groceries instead of the sea filling our net with fish, we would not have stopped to share the story of richness that filled our day. Fish farms and hatcheries, like groceries stores, reflect stories of human ingenuity, stories of things built and profits earned. Wild salmon swimming into our lives spawn an awareness of the generosity upon which all of our lives depend.

The artists lifting stone tools to cave walls lived with a keen awareness of this generosity. Salmon coursed through their imaginations, their bodies, their lives. For the vast stretch of years since that fisherman on the French coast finished his work and walked out of the cave, humans have lived close to the cycles of the earth; we have felt the hunger of winter, welcomed the warmth of spring, celebrated the return of fish.

Just as a plant community can tap the intelligence stored with its collective DNA, human culture navigates the future steered by the wisdom stored within our collective stories and experiences. The increasing disappearance of salmon from the streams of Europe and rivers of the Eastern Seaboard and, more recently, the watersheds of the West Coast, take with them far more than the nourishment of their flesh. Along with the dwindling fish, experiences are lost and stories fade. And as the annual splash and pulse of fish slip away, the breadth and agility and wisdom of our culture is diminished. For the French children growing up today on the banks of the Vézère River, the fish etched onto the cave wall is frozen in stone, inert, with no living mirror leaping and splashing through the light of day.

From the dense forest of Alaska's panhandle to the sparse tundra of the North Slope, almost all Alaskan children grow up within a few miles of a salmon stream. The education those kids get once summer vacation begins and the salmon return keeps alive a precious, shimmering swath of our cultural imagination. The vibrant, vigorous multitudes of salmon surging through our northern rivers remind us that every breath we take, every calorie we consume, is a gift from this earth.

To forget this does not make it less so.

When I first came to Alaska in 1975, the pipeline was being built and jobs were plentiful, but I had been reading Jack London stories and Robert Service poetry and wanted an adventure. I got a job as a stewardess for Yutana Barge Lines working on the boats that push barges up and down the Tanana and Yukon Rivers. It was an adventure from start to finish. I will never forget my first taste of dried salmon from Holy Cross. It was love at first chew! Later in my life our children teethed on this delicacy. That Holy Cross fish was the beginning of my lifelong love of salmon—fishing for it, eating it, and sharing it with friends and family

Renamary Rauchenstein
Talkeetna

Salmon Are Worth More Than Money
CHARLES WOHLFORTH

Charles Wohlforth, a resident of Anchorage and Kachemak Bay, is the author of ten books. This essay draws on ideas developed in his book *The Fate of Nature: Rediscovering Our Ability to Rescue the Earth.*

MOST ALASKANS CARE ABOUT SALMON for more than the obvious reasons. We love to eat them. We love to sell them. But we eat and sell a lot of things without believing they define the place we live and the way we live here. Even salmon doesn't mean so much if it comes from a Styrofoam package in a grocery store, especially if it was raised in a pen. Salmon matters most when it connects us to our place.

Human beings are emotional beasts. Often, intangibles matter more to us than money. Our relationships. Our homes. Some people love money more than anything else. Most of us hold those people in contempt.

It's odd, then, that we see fisheries almost exclusively through the lens of money. Permits that commercial fishermen buy and sell give them the right to catch and sell fish. Guides and tourism businesses fight to bring fish into the rivers like swimming paychecks coming home. Even subsistence and personal use fishermen often talk about the avoided cost of food. All have a personal relationship to salmon, but that's usually not the topic of discussion. It's usually about who gets how much of the economic take.

Don't these fish, and the ecosystem that produces them, mean more to us that the material wealth they provide? And how did we adopt the language of private property for the free-swimming salmon, that potent symbol of the wild?

Alaska became a state in large part because of the belief that Alaskans could do a better job of protecting salmon runs than the federal government, which mismanaged salmon harvests into a desperate scarcity in the first half of the twentieth century. But the early years after statehood were no better. Too many fishermen chased too few fish. Only after the state was more than a decade old, and with a state constitutional amendment, did a limited entry system come into force that would hold down the number of commercial fishermen and give each a vested interest in enhancing the total size of the catch.

Not everyone liked the idea. Jay Hammond, not yet governor, was one early opponent. Always attuned to the impact of new laws on village Alaska, Jay saw risk in handing out property deeds to a wild resource that had been owned by all. He feared Alaska Natives could become alienated from the food resource that had always sustained them. Unfortunately, he was right. Although Native communities got extra consideration when permits were allocated in the 1970s, the decades since have seen many villages lose permits. These permits are valuable assets, easily sold during hard times, taken by the IRS, or put on the market through the life events that affect every family. In cash-poor communities, the permits are unlikely to return.

Non-Native Alaskans also saw their relationship to fisheries change when new laws assigned fish ownership. In salmon fisheries, the boat and permit owners got older. Young fishermen had to work a long time before they could afford permits of their own. More fishermen listed addresses from cities and areas Outside, fewer from Alaska's coastal towns.

Many such private stories have accumulated to become the statistics kept by the State's Commercial Fisheries Entry Commission. Since the system started in 1974, the number of permits owned by rural residents for fishing from their own communities declined from 8,219 to 5,987. In Bristol

Bay, locals with salmon drift permits declined by 352 while non-Alaskans gained 285 of those permits and urban Alaskans 43 of them. In 2000, Dillingham had 274 permit holders; ten years later, the number had dwindled to 227.

The system of individual fishing quotas (known as IFQs) for federally managed species such as halibut and cod had an even more dramatic impact, dividing fish from communities that used to rely upon them. Anthropologists writing for the American Fisheries Society in 2008 reported coastal communities with new classes of haves and have-nots, depending on who was lucky enough to get fishing quota shares when they were handed out, or rich enough to buy them after the system started.

Another unintended consequence of permit ownership came about because the private property idea worked too well. As intended, limited entry permits did provide a financial interest in the health of the total catch. Fishermen invested in hatcheries, and within a decade of the system being in place catch numbers exploded.

But more salmon isn't always a good thing. There's a limit to how many predatory fish an ocean ecosystem can sustain. There's good evidence that wild runs suffered when huge numbers of hatchery fish entered the ocean. There's also evidence that ocean ecosystems can be reordered in new, less resilient ways when they are overwhelmed by hatchery salmon; other species that occupy the same roles in the food web are displaced, and that reduction in diversity yields a less robust system.

The ecosystem evidence isn't very strong, however, and there's another, related reason for that. Biologists don't study those other fish much. They focus on the money fish, the salmon that bring fishermen's paydays and fish tax receipts. It's almost as if non-commercial species don't exist, for the lack of attention from scientists monitoring Alaska's coastal ecosystems.

What's wrong with that? Maybe nothing, if all we care about is eating and selling salmon. But if we care about the place, the ecosystem, the wild salmon, and how the fish relate to our cultures, our communities, and our sense of ourselves, then there is something wrong with severing the fish from anything but its economic value.

We live in an economic and political system that teaches us to think in certain ways. Many cultures through history and prehistory have subsisted cooperatively and sustainably on shared natural resources without creating schemes of private ownership. Our system of free enterprise and representative government doesn't account for that. Our solutions depend on economic and political competition—on the dual struggles to make money and make laws. Private ownership often seems like the only way to incentivize conservation in our dog-eat-dog world.

But if we want to keep coastal ecosystems intact, and coastal people an essential part of them, we need new ways of thinking about our relationship to nature. We need to manage ecosystems in whole, not only the money fish. We need to value the relationship of an entire community to the sea, not only the people who stand to cash in.

In the end, a more holistic approach will benefit everyone—including the fishermen. Because hazards threatening the oceans now are much larger than fishermen can handle alone. They need the rest of us.

In the global economic arena, fishing is a puny industry. Oil, mining, and the myriad industries contributing to climate change and ocean acidification are immeasurably mightier. If the Pebble Mine prospect is worth as much as they say, the owners could buy all the gillnet permits in Bristol Bay for a tenth of a percent the ore's worth. Through the lens of money, salmon lose.

Economically, the world can do without fishing entirely. We don't even need fishermen to supply seafood restaurants: many diners actually prefer farmed salmon. If the only reason to save wild salmon is because of its economic value, then the battle is probably lost.

But I don't think money is the reason to save salmon runs, or ever was. Most Alaskans would like to know healthy wild salmon runs will be swimming up our rivers a century from now. Not because we will be eating them or selling them. We'll all be dead by then. We care about the children who come after us and the lives they will lead. What was good for us we want to be good for them.

As an economic resource, salmon are transitory, like everything that rises and falls in the market of buying and selling. But these wants are not economic. If we save salmon, it will be because we fulfilled our deeper hopes for the world. It will be because we cared enough to save something we loved.

At the age of eighteen, I made my way across the country from New York, catching rides with friends and hitchhiking a ride on a salmon tender from Seattle to Kodiak to work in a cannery. My long days of work in salmon and crab canneries put me through engineering school and paid for a semester off to travel the world. I met my husband, a commercial fisherman, while working in a salmon cannery. We've been married now for over twenty-seven years—and have literally caught tons of fish! We own a commercial salmon setnet business in Prince William Sound, where we've raised our kids and taught them to catch salmon and to work hard as a family toward a common goal. We were Fishing for Tuition! Our setnet site has paid for both our children to go to college. Our son loves salmon fishing so much that he bought his own setnet site in Prince William Sound. When we aren't commercial salmon fishing, we're usually off sportfishing for salmon and other treats of the sea, mending our nets, or repairing equipment for the next season.

Susan Harvey
Eagle River

Salmon have been central to nearly everything I do, my whole life. I grew up seining and setnetting for salmon around Kodiak and even worked at a cannery for a short stint. I learned to fly-fish at a young age, and salmon fishing always provides me a valuable escape. I studied fisheries in college, which led to a career with the Alaska Department of Fish and Game. I conducted a project on migrating salmon as a graduate student and then became a full-time research biologist. As my biology career evolved, I took yet another salmon-related path by developing a salmon jerky. With a friend, I built a small seafood processing company to produce and market the salmon jerky. We sponsored several Olympic and professional athletes fueled by our salmon product and made a nationally broadcast television commercial. Most recently, I've become an artist, and salmon are one of my main subjects. Salmon have been an integral part of all facets of my life. If that isn't salmon love, I don't know what is!

Mark Witteveen
Kodiak

What Happens in the Arctic?

DEBBY DAHL EDWARDSON

Debby Dahl Edwardson lives and writes from Barrow, Alaska. Debby's books have earned starred reviews and have been named to many lists including the International Reading Association's Best Books for a Global Society and ALA/YALSA's Best Fiction for Young Adults. Her most recent book, *My Name Is Not Easy*, was a finalist for the National Book Award and was chosen to represent Alaska at the Library of Congress.

THE YEAR WAS 1981. It was an oil hearing in Barrow. In those days the oil hearings were an ongoing event. Every week, it seemed, they were taking testimony on yet another Environmental Impact Statement (EIS), and they always had translators because the majority of the people testifying spoke in Inupiaq. The people, all of them, spoke against offshore development. The sea, they said, was their garden.

Don't drill in our garden, they said. *Don't drill on our dinner table.*

The hearings were aired on the radio, the Inupiaq testimony translated into English, hour after hour. In those days, one could learn the language by listening to the radio.

It was summer, and the ice had broken up and moved offshore just enough to allow room for boating, the way it always did. Hunters were out in their boats, weaving in and out of the ice floes, following spotted and bearded seals—*natchiq* and *ugruk*—late into the serenity of the midnight sun.

People had tents and cabins north of town at Piġniq, where they always set nets this time of year to catch *aanaakliq*, "whitefish"; *qalugruaq*, "dog salmon"; and *amaqtuuq*, "humpback salmon."

The names of fish, land animals, and sea mammals were among the first words I learned in Inupiaq. It was not difficult for even a relative newcomer to see the importance of the land, the sea, and their resources to the people of Barrow. If I didn't know what subsistence meant when I first moved north, I learned it quickly. I learned it when I found subsistence gifts on my doorstep—a few fish, a caribou leg, seal meat, or a piece of maktak. Subsistence resources are shared resources.

There was a young man testifying at the hearing I was listening to on that particular day, and his testimony made me sit up. Speaking in village English, he tore the latest EIS to pieces, page by page. Clearly this guy had done his homework. He ended with this statement: "We have said no as individuals; we have said no as communities. We have said no as regional tribal governments, and in Point Thompson, we said no as a total Alaska Native people. And we have also said no on an international level. Through our Inuit Circumpolar Conference we said no. What does it take to make that be understood? We have said no in every forum we can. Has the meaning of that word changed?"

Listening to the articulate, measured anger simmering just beneath the surface of this man's words made me feel sorry for the oil industry that day. Almost.

I married that man. His name is George Edwardson and he was, at the time, working as natural resource director for the Inupiat Community of the Arctic Slope, the tribal government that serves a region the size of Minnesota. He later became its president.

When people ask me how long I've lived in Barrow, I've taken to telling them this: I've lived here all my adult life. I was a very young and somewhat foolish woman when I moved north, and I am now considered an elder, or an elder-in-training as we say here. I've lived here the majority of my life, in other words, and have seen changes of a magnitude barely believable when I think of it. Sometimes thinking of it depresses me unbearably, as though I've witnessed the passing of a way of life, precious beyond words, hard though it often was.

At a conference I attended in Anchorage recently, I watched a young Barrow hunter narrate a presentation full of Barrow photos. When he came to the photo that showed the iconic view of Barrow in the summer, the one with huge chunks of ice bobbing in the water just offshore, he paused. "This is what it used to look like."

Now, in the summer, the ice moves offshore quickly, hundreds of miles out of sight, leaving the coast of Barrow as ice free as Hawaii. This, alone, scares me. It scares me because the first thing I always think is this: what becomes of the people of the Arctic, the people who have built a technology, a complex linguistic system, and a way of survival based on their knowledge of ice—what becomes of the Inupiat when the ice is gone?

Don't worry about us, my husband says. *We have survived seven ice ages. We have watched the warming and freezing of the planet seven times. We will survive.*

The changes I've seen, the changes that young hunter has seen—these pale next to those my husband has witnessed. My husband comes from the days of dogsleds, kerosene lamps, and candles. He remembers his first set of store-bought clothes. He knows exactly how many walrus, how many salmon, and what kind, were needed to fuel a dog team. Back before the days of snow machines.

I remember vividly the day I first arrived in Barrow. It was early February, bright with the brilliance of returned sun on pristine snow: the coldest time of the year here, in other words. Huge piles of crystal-line ice—Barrow's drinking water—were stacked in front of the homes, glistening in the bright cold sun with a kind of magic. The first meal I tasted, dark and thick, was *tutu* soup. I'll never forget the surprise of its rich flavor, eaten in fellowship with a strong, laughing, and remarkably humble people, a people clearly of the land, the forbidding and beautiful Arctic land.

Tutu, "caribou," is one of those words one always says in Inupiaq, even today. There are others, many others. Still.

In those days I learned to sew skin clothing, the essential survival gear of the Arctic, from the elder seamstresses of Barrow, all gone now; the women who could make a pattern just by looking at you, who could trim the legs of caribou, wolves, and polar bear exactly right for mukluks. The ones who could make hoods that always fit perfectly even in the strongest of winds. Making a hood fit perfectly in these conditions is a true art, believe me.

I dreamed, in those days, of having an Arctic entry, a *qanitchuq*, lined with Barrow-style parkas I'd made myself.

Today we have full plumbing and even a dishwasher. I have a reverse osmosis water system under my sink, and our drinking water comes from a little spout. We order everything from books to hunting gear on the Internet. And although I have never fully mastered the art of the hood, I do have a *qanitchuq* full of the parkas I've made. And in the dead of winter, we do still need them.

But most important, the subsistence heart of this culture, this people of the land, still beats just as strong as it ever did.

When our kids were young we taught them the time-honored tradition of sharing their first subsistence catch with an elder. Now that we are elders ourselves, my husband and I are often the recipients of this largesse. A few weeks ago it was polar bear meat from a nephew. Before that it was caribou from a great-niece, and in the summer it is always fresh fish from the nets people still set at Piġniq.

I remember being surprised and tickled the first time someone brought me a couple of salmon. I hadn't considered this to be salmon country. In truth, the Inupiat have always caught salmon. My husband says this was part of the food that sustained the dogs in winters of subzero temperatures. It was a lot of work to catch the food that the dogs—and their people—survived on. It was all part of a cycle, a cycle that people were—are—part of, even as things change and species, including the human species, evolve.

When I worked at Ilisagvik College, the North Slope's tribal college, I ran a program aimed at training marine mammal observers. The MMOs are the local people the industry has agreed to take on board as observers under the terms of what was initially dubbed the oiler-whaler agreement and is now known officially as the Open Water Season Conflict Avoidance Agreement. Under this agreement, local MMOs are hired to watch out for the welfare of marine mammals. Their reports are supposed to have the authority to halt industrial activity in areas where animals are present, although in reality—as I learned from firsthand reports of my students— the MMOs are not always well used. An animal seen is not always reported in the ship's log. The spray of a whale is interpreted as the splashing of waves, for example, and goes unreported.

My husband's cousin Puvuk was an MMO. He reported seeing a large group of *aivgit,* "walrus," on an ice floe. It's a common sight here, so common there's even a word for it, a word even I know: *nunavak.* It refers to a herd of walrus packed up together into a tight brown cluster on an ice floe, making the ice look, from a distance, like a piece of land, or *nuna.* The scientists on board the ship where Puvuk was working that time refused to believe, at first, that the landmark they saw before them wasn't an island.

The Inupiat have a long history of teaching scientists about the Arctic. They also have a long history of helping scientists understand and find ways to explain, in terms of western science, things already well documented in traditional knowledge systems.

As part of the MMO training program at Ilisagvik, I developed a traditional knowledge track and always invited elders to visit the class to talk about their knowledge of the Arctic Ocean. Now, just a few years later, virtually all of the elder hunters I invited to speak to my students are gone.

One of those elders—one considered a true expert of the land and sea—was Arnold Brower Sr., one of my husband's own teachers. What he said to my students the day he spoke to them floored me. He said he could no longer tell them, with complete confidence, about the ways of the Arctic Ocean. The ocean was changing too fast, changing with unprecedented speed. New species are moving north, he said. Changing ice and water conditions are rewriting the behavior patterns of those animals that have always lived here.

The implications of this are stunning. I think, for example, of the fall when a hundred polar bears were stranded on shore when the ice moved out too far, too suddenly, for them to follow. I think, too, of the summer we watched a *nanuq*, a "polar bear," running up inland. Where was he going and why?

Don't worry about the nanuq, my husband always says. *The nanuq will survive and evolve.* They are already mating with *aklat*, the "brown bears." They do this, my husband says, in order to have their young learn the way of the land because they know what's coming.

So much has changed and is changing in the Arctic, but one thing that remains firmly unchanged is this: my husband is still speaking out against offshore development. People no longer speak in unison on this subject, and they no longer speak largely in Inupiaq. These were impacts predicted in the 1982 EIS report:

> Regional significant impacts on socio-cultural systems in the form of political and social unrest, conflict and dissension are probable during the projected life of the field . . . expected harmful reactions may include accelerated rates of crime, alcohol, drug abuse, violence, apathy and alienation, particularly in Barrow.

We are seeing those impacts today.

What happens in the Arctic Ocean affects one-third of the world's fisheries, my husband says. He is talking about the salmon. He is citing evidence that suggests the salmon are moving north in increasing numbers. He mentions a friend of ours who witnessed, while working as an MMO, huge schools of salmon fingerlings in the waters along the Arctic Coast.

The salmon are moving north.

Who will protect this renewable resource—a resource that, like the whales, seals, walrus, and polar bear, is somehow never figured into the equation of industrial development and its impacts? How can they measure the impact of development on a resource they have not yet fully assessed— not in these waters, at any rate?

I learned from my husband the Inupiaq way of looking at the world more than thirty years ago. It was a good way of seeing things, and it's given me a good life. We've raised seven children on subsistence resources. Subsistence was critical to their health. They ate fish *quaq*, "frozen fish with seal oil," at least once a week when they were growing up. The gifts of subsistence sustained us in a fashion our meager income never could have.

When I think of it now, I realize something I've never had reason to think of: there is no Inupiaq word for subsistence. There is no word because a word is not needed. Subsistence is implied in the Inupiaq way of life, in the very fiber of what it means to be Inupiaq. Subsistence—a slippery word at best in English—is no less than the natural order of life in Inupiaq. It includes, not insignificantly, all the important values one needs to survive as a human being, the values we here at the top of the world call the Inupiaq Values: sharing, compassion, cooperation, avoidance of conflict, love and respect for our elders and one another, humor, humility, family and kinship, knowledge of language, hunting traditions, spirituality, and respect for nature.

Those values taken in aggregate imply something quite simple and profound. All living creatures, human and animal—mammal, fish, and fowl alike—are interdependent, part of the cycle of life. If we take care of the animals, the land, and each other, these will take care of us, because people, too, are a part of the ecosystem—that's how the Inupiat have always seen it, that's what a subsistence life teaches us. No one here has to spell it out: it's just the way it is.

It's all connected. Whether or not salmon survive to sustain the rest of the world, maintaining their critical role in the ecosystem, depends a great deal on what happens here, right here in the Arctic.

Taavra. That's all.

My husband, Chad, and I have been commercial beach seining in the Kodiak area for five years now. As we go into our sixth year we have done some reflection and realize that fishing is what is keeping us here in our hometown of Larsen Bay. If it weren't for fishing we believe we would have moved away from the island. The high price of fuel in the village and the cost to freight things in make it hard to live here, and we've learned that we need to rely on the resources around us. We have three young children. All three love fishing, love being on the boat, and can't wait until the fishing season begins. Salmon are our way of life!

Alice Aga
Larsen Bay

The Right Kind of Hungry

JULIA O'MALLEY

Julia O'Malley is a freelance journalist and the Atwood Chair of Journalism at the University of Alaska Anchorage. Previously, she spent nine years at the *Anchorage Daily News* as a reporter and columnist. She lives in Anchorage and blogs about food and culture in Alaska at juliaomalley.media.

I WILL GIVE YOU MY SALMON RECIPE. It is simple, delicious, and particularly impressive considering some of the not impressive salmon recipes in my genetic code. Take my grandmother's, which I won't give you, not because it is secret, but because I can't encourage cooking in a dishwasher. All I'm going to say is that it involves Saran Wrap, the top rack, and the sanitize cycle.

Some of my eight uncles and aunts on my father's side, the older ones, say the dishwasher story can't be true. But others, the younger ones, saw it with their own eyes. It's weird, sure, but, they told me, the fish comes out of the dishwasher impossibly tender. And that's what everybody wants.

My parents tell me that when they were growing up in the little town that was Anchorage in the late 1950s and early '60s, people didn't eat grilled salmon all summer long the way we all do now. Certainly, some people fished. Some people smoked salmon or canned it. But it wasn't usual to find fresh salmon in the grocery stores. Salmon wasn't the go-to. It wasn't as common as, say, frozen fillet of sole purchased at the commissary, which was served at the O'Malley house on Fridays with regularity.

When I think about eating salmon, dinner at Aunt Barbara's house is the first thing that comes to mind. Aunt Barbara, number two in the line-up of O'Malley children (Dad is number three), somehow became a devoted fisherwoman. Devoted may be the wrong word. Zealous might be better. She likes nothing better than to be photographed with a bloody fish in her embrace. And unlike her mother, my grandmother, she knows how to cook it.

Barbara's table is where I often taste the first catch of the season. Many years it is spring king, thick and fatty. Her fish recipe, like mine, is simple, a variation on one you find all across Alaska. It involves a splash of soy sauce and perhaps thin rounds of lemon and a sprinkle of dill. The fish goes to the grill on a sheet of foil. Always, it is eaten around a crowded table, always with rice, hot sourdough bread, butter, steamed broccoli, and hollandaise sauce.

Summer in Alaska is like no other place. You might compare the feeling of spring coming on to that of driving a really nice car off a car lot, a car that you bought outright with your own money after years spent riding a bus. There is a grand sense of liberation as the light returns and crocus buds appear, an intoxicated appreciation for all that is green and alive. If that feeling could have a flavor, it would be salmon, perfectly cooked, hot off the grill. The perfectly cooked part is harder than it seems, but stay with me, I can help.

Fresh salmon is Alaska's food, our most famous culinary export, one of our few proud flags on the world's food map. Alaska Airlines flies the first batch of Copper River reds to Seattle in a "Salmon-Thirty-Salmon" jet, painted to look like a king salmon. Photos move on the Associated Press wire soon after: a fat, cold fish being carried down a red carpet to a line of chefs on the Seattle tarmac. The fish soon appears on menus of the country's finest restaurants and in the seafood cases at Whole Foods. The price of Copper River salmon in the spring might easily top thirty dollars a pound.

But in Alaska, exquisite fish isn't that rare or expensive. In fact, it is free once you get to a place where you can catch it. In Anchorage, anybody with a pole can walk to Ship Creek downtown and come away with a bright fish. The beaches of the Kenai River, the closest dipnet fishery to Anchorage, draw scores of city people, many from Anchorage's new and growing ethnic communities who join the crowd of longtime fishermen with their waders and long-handled nets. On a short walk along the shore you can hear Samoan, Tagalog, Korean, Thai, Vietnamese, Lao, Hmong, and Spanish. On any given night in Anchorage in the summertime, salmon is roasting on a thousand grills, it's being rolled into sushi and flaked into tacos. Salmon here is the people's food. And so long as our rivers and oceans remain healthy, everyone can be fed.

I've pulled in exactly one salmon in my thirty-six years. I was sixteen and Aunt Barbara was my guide. We rose early to drive to the Kasilof River, listening to oldies on the radio until we got out of range. Aunt Barbara chain-smoked. We ate nothing except a roll of Sweet Tarts. Fishing on a full stomach = bad luck.

Following Barb was an education in superstitious fish rituals. As I drove, I shared the front seat with two cantaloupes. When we arrived at the home of the guide who would pilot us downriver, Barbara gave him the melons. I knew enough to understand it was not so much a gesture of friendliness as an offering.

Barbara thought hard before selecting a seat in the open skiff, her mind working through the various traits of other lucky seats in other boats. She went left side, close to the guide. Soon we set off into the river and drifted dreamily for several hours, the guide gently rowing as we bounced our hooks on the river floor, each baited with a cluster of hot-pink eggs.

Then, like a lightning strike, came a tug. You can't forget that sensation, the pleasure of the weight at the end of the line and the wave of adrenaline. The boat came alive, everybody shouting to *set the hook!* and *reel-reel-reel!* I did my best. Soon the fish appeared, first a flash of sliver, then a ribbon of muscle just beneath the surface. In a flurry of shouting and netting, it was in with us. Eyes wide. Needle teeth. Red fans visible inside the gill flaps. If I remember correctly, after some coaching, I clubbed it myself. I totally enjoyed every minute of that trip, but I have a secret: I have never had much of a desire to catch a fish again.

There is no complicated reason why. I'd just much rather spend my time with fish cooking and eating it.

It's hard to be Alaskan and feel this way. I concealed it for many years. When I first met my wife, Sara, fourteen years ago, I spent hours in her skiff off Douglas Island near Juneau, circling in the water, motor purring, trolling for salmon. Her boat was called *Fish Wife,* and I watched her expertly back it down the ramp into the water with awe.

She was always the one with the lucky seat, pulling in fish after fish. Meanwhile, as if the fish could sense my lack of interest, I never got much more than a nibble. She kept her fillet knife sharp, and I watched her pull it through our catch over and over that summer, skimming it along the backbone, making a precise cut through the silver scales.

My fish recipe starts at this moment.

The fish, to be perfect, must be impossibly fresh, preferably hours from the water, or even less. It must be filleted almost immediately, with confidence and a knife so sharp, if you were to slip, it would slice you to the bone.

Everybody has a favorite kind of salmon. Some like fatty, increasingly hard-to-get king in the springtime; others, mellow silver in the fall. I like red salmon best, specifically from the Copper River, with flesh the color and translucency of ripe highbush cranberries.

This isn't the easiest fish to obtain. It must be netted from a swift, cold river hours away from town.

I might love reds best because I grew up eating them. Back then, we relied on my uncle Bob for fish. He is the husband of my mother's sister Alicia. He is British and old enough to remember World War II.

He was a petroleum engineer who came to Alaska to work for ARCO during the pipeline.

Bob packed to go fishing meticulously. His tidy lists, written in pencil, sat on the counter until each item was checked off. I remember coolers marked with duct tape labels and what seemed to be an entire duffle bag filled with peanut M&Ms.

Sometime after he'd left, a call would come in with the number of fish he'd netted. Dozens often, but sometimes none. The possibility of failure made the catch all the more precious.

If he got a haul, then there was an assembly line in the kitchen, fillet after fillet, packed into bags, vacuum-sealed, frozen. A few fillets would be distributed among the family. And always, afterward, a big fishing victory dinner. A salad of romaine dressed with balsamic. Grilled zucchini. The salmon marinated in Yoshida's teriyaki sauce or coated with olive oil and a shake of Tony Chachere's Creole seasoning.

Soon afterward, Alicia would start up the Little Chief smoker in the yard.

Alicia died years ago, but Bob still goes to the Copper. Now the next generation of the family makes the trip. Sara goes. So does my cousin's husband, John. They stay up all night waiting for the rush of fish. Sometimes they tie themselves to the bank to guard against the current.

When Sara gets home, her dad comes over and they set up a table in the driveway, cleaning, filleting, and rinsing each fish with the garden hose. Then the fillets come to me. I pack the bags and run the vacuum sealer, just like Alicia did, whirring in the kitchen well into the never-dark night. I put some into the freezer, but the majority we give away.

Fish is best when eaten fresh (in fact, I don't really like it frozen), and so I'd rather just share it. Maybe that is my superstitious fish ritual. Fresh fish is my offering, given away in hopes that I might get some in return later, when I am without. So far, it has worked.

My cousin Tanya, Bob and Alicia's daughter and John's wife, has an amazing way with fish. She makes salmon poke, a Hawaiian-style delicacy:

raw fish, straight from the freezer, cubed and mixed with tamari, sesame oil, chili paste, and onions. That recipe is killer, but her best recipe begins with a fresh fillet, hot off the grill, smothered with fresh-chopped green onions. She drizzles hot peanut oil over it. You can hear the oil sizzle as it hits the fish and wilts the onions. She follows that with a splash of hot soy sauce. Serve this with sticky rice from the Vietnamese restaurant down the street and you can't top it. This is almost my favorite salmon recipe, but not quite.

If I am being honest, my salmon recipe isn't really even mine, it's Sara's. The first time I ate it was all those years ago on North Douglas Island, after one of our circular tours on the *Fish Wife*. We took our hour-old fish back to the house and made a round of calls to invite friends to dinner. And then we started up the grill. It was propane, with cast-iron grates, wire brushed as clean as possible and well-seasoned with oil. This is, in my opinion, the best way to cook. I never let fresh fish near an oven.

I have learned the methods Sara taught me. Always give the grill time to develop a nice even heat but don't put the fire on full blast. It should be heated to medium, so that your hand can hover over the grates for just a few seconds before it becomes too uncomfortable.

Next put the fish on a sheet pan. Pour a capful of olive oil over it and generously sprinkle it with sea salt. That's it. When the grill is ready, lay the fillet directly on the grate, skin side down. Close the top.

Seems simple, right? Don't be fooled. Next comes the hardest and most essential part of my recipe. It is not an ingredient, but technique: to experience the sacred deliciousness of fresh salmon, impossibly moist, and perfect, you must not overcook it. This is really hard.

Everybody overcooks fish. That changes the flavors of its delicate oils and the texture. Done wrong, fish is flaky and bitter. People eat so much like this, they become accustomed. It is the norm. They don't know what they are missing. Done right, grilled fresh salmon's texture is closer to custard, its flavor mild, sweet, and faintly briny.

I can't give you a cooking time once you have the fish on the grill, because every fish is a different size, but the key is to be vigilant. Err on the side of rawness. Also, for the fish to taste most delicious, you have to be the right kind of hungry. You should be hungry the way you only get in May, on a day when the sun feels warm and you can smell sap, and teenagers skateboard by with no coats on. It should have been months since you last had a piece of salmon. You'll know it's right, because you'll smell your neighbors grilling, too, for the first time since last year.

You'll want to grill some asparagus, too. And set a pan of rice going on the stove.

You might stand at the grill in flip-flops on grass that isn't quite greened up. (You are free to do this with a beer in your hand.) Check the fish just about the time you start to notice your feet are cold, because even though it's sunny, there is still a chill. If you've hit it right, you can tell, because when you take a fork and slip it between the layers of flesh, you will see that in the center of the fish it is not quite done and is instead just slightly translucent. With a long spatula, separate the fish from the skin on the grill. Place it on a warm plate. Serve immediately.

Salmon is our elders' favorite and is also a part of our culture. In my hometown we go ice fishing, fall fishing, and summer fishing. During ice fishing we use ice hooks made of wood (made by hand) and make round holes into the ice. Most days there are up to ten people ice fishing, all dressed warm in their parkas or jackets. Fall fishing is seining, where everyone uses a long fishing net. This is where they catch most of the fish. People go in boats and share their catch by dividing it to each other. They freeze them outside to make "aged" fish. Summer fishing we catch salmon or trout. It is a good time because of all the scenery and good weather. Salmon is everyone's favorite, and I'm happy we can go fishing just a few miles from our home.

Sonja Barger
Kivalina

I have been taught as a very young child by my parents and grandparents to care and process our salmon. We take special measures to carefully catch, split, smoke, jar, salt, freeze. I have been blessed that my parents have passed down their knowledge to my children. It is our love of salmon that feeds us during the long cold winter days.

Martha Anelon
Iliamna

Seasons

ERNESTINE HAYES

Ernestine Hayes is a member of the Kaagwaantaan clan of the Tlingit. Author of *Blonde Indian: An Alaska Native Memoir* and other published works, Hayes teaches composition and creative writing at the University of Alaska Southeast in her hometown of Juneau.

IN THE PART OF THE WORLD THAT IS LINGIT AANI, "Southeast Alaska," the histories and the futures of the people and the salmon are woven together.

The original people of this part of the world count their histories by the movement of the glaciers. Along with the movement of the glaciers comes the movement of the salmon. Along with the salmon come the seasons and the tides. In, out. Back, forth. Leave, return. Leave. Return.

After the end of summer, after the summer's rush, when everything has been gathered and stored and collected against the coming winter, all anyone can do is wait. Count the firewood, ponder the weather, await the coming night.

When people become still, they hear the life-filled forest and the life-filled ocean preparing themselves for the coming cold. Enough of summer's romance: hemlock and spruce now tuck their hands to their bellies. Clouds now mask the moon. Berry bushes, no longer charming, spend their attention on turning their last few fruits into seeds. Even the mosses cease their creeping.

All these living things know they will lose ground, vigor, life before the time comes to press forward again. In the meantime, they can only wait.

Some generations ago, there came a white tide that threatened the people who are original to this part of the world. The places where they live and move were mistreated, damaged, destroyed, and taken from them. The people themselves were harmed, their numbers weakened, their health reduced. They were displaced, their belongings diminished. They were forced to abandon their original homes. Where once they were rich and powerful, in only a generation or two most of their power and wealth were made no more than memories.

With the growing white tide, true history became difficult to keep. Language and style and fashion and fishing grounds and smokehouse sites and clan property and family keepsakes and *at.oow* and indeed the very spirits with which the coming generations had always been entrusted and called upon to provide for and nurture and keep warm and protect were all but forgotten.

The original people were told they must speak the new language. They were told they must wear the new clothes. They were told they must gather from the ocean for profit and not for balance, and they must look upon fish as things and not as salmon-people. They were told they must join the white tide. They were told they must obtain the new form of education and they must teach themselves this new way of thinking. They were told they must associate being successful and being educated and being modern with the new white tide. They were told that they owed it to their futures to turn away from the teachings of the past.

And thus it came about that winter fell upon the people and collapsed the many generations.

After some years, the original people became weakened and sickened and were almost overwhelmed, whereupon great interest was born in the hearts of those who had come with the white tide. The very idea of original people stirred curiosity and even dedication in the hearts of the white tide people. The white tide people pledged to devote their lives to saving what was left, and they pledged to re-create what they felt could not be saved.

The white tide people began to study everything about the original people. They became authorities on everything about the original people. They spoke of the original people, and they spoke about the original people, and they spoke for the original people. They wrote books about the original people and awarded themselves degrees on the study of the original people. They sat on panels and lectured in halls. The white tide people taught the original people about themselves and revered the very idea of original people.

In the middle of these generations, throughout the passing years, there were those of the original people who harbored the constant hope that their lives and their deaths would provide sustenance and strength to coming generations in the same ways that their salmon relatives provided sustenance and strength to their generations.

The seasons turned and turned again, and the original people harbored a constant, deep hunger every time the wind whispered hints of approaching dark. In every darkest season, the original people continued to raise their voices to call out for dryfish, and they treasured the seaweed and berries and all the riches stored alongside the fragrant dryfish that sustained them until the spring arrived. And more important, they treasured the riches that were carried to each winter's celebrations so that everyone would be made aware that their wealth and their generosity and their generations were imperishable.

Some generations ago, the salmon of this part of the world with whom the original people identify and upon which so much of their wealth once relied were so great in number that they thickened the streams. But the places where the salmon once lived and moved have been damaged, destroyed, taken. The salmon of this part of the world have been harmed; their numbers have been weakened; their health has been reduced.

Now the white tide people study the salmon and bemoan the loss. They speak of the salmon, and they speak about the salmon, and they speak for the salmon. They write books about the salmon and award themselves degrees in the study of salmon. They sit on panels and lecture in halls. The white tide people revere the very idea of what salmon once were, and they have pledged to save what is left.

In this part of the world, the history of the original people and the history of the salmon are woven together.

Even when summers are finished, all people in this part of the world know they must remain vigilant. All people know that our relatives, the bears and the wolves, are eager to add one more layer to their stored fat, preparing for the coming cold just as they must do.

Shallow borders that invite sunlight along the shore soon have scant purpose. Open spaces soon reveal only gray shadows, and then for only the briefest portion of the day. The inviting smells of the wet forest are soon covered with the blanket of snow that keeps everything safe and fresh and alive until the time comes for rebirth.

As winter approaches, it is time for all the people in this part of the world to build up more nourishment than at first would seem to be needed. As winter approaches, it is time to collect and dry or smoke or jar the last of the fish from the waters and to preserve the berries and roots and greens from the generous land.

And now, the original people of this part of the world have declared that they will become healthy. They have determined that they will regain their own language; they will educate their own children; they will lift up their own scholars. They have offered to share their ways of knowing, and the white tide people have now resolved that they will listen and all will go forward in the same season.

In this part of the world, the futures of all the people and all the salmon are woven together.

Fly-fishing has a purity of form to me. But purity often comes with struggle. I had spent hours fishing, hoping for coho to take my Dalai Lama streamer and eight-weight line for a pull through salt flats. With each cast and stripping of line comes the heart-beating hope that this cast, this strip, this moment, one of these fish will hit your fly and take off until you're down to your backing, your knuckles bashed from trying to palm your reel.

Again, I cast out and let the fly swing. Two strips. One last slow strip. Then I felt it. I pulled back, as aggressively as I could be with thirty feet of line out. The fish jumped. Jumped again. Ran. The reel whined. As I was smiling, I realized I was down to my backing. I adjusted the drag and pulled the fish in.

When I saw the fish, I understood it was giving me two gifts: the pleasure of connecting with something that had spent four years to get back home, and also food. The salmon is a creature that comes around to feed everyone: the streams, the trees, the bears, the birds, and, of course, me and my family.

Christopher Orman
Juneau

One morning, when I was still new to Bethel, I was leaving my apartment for work and found an ice chest filled with fresh filleted salmon outside my door. It was a nice surprise after just surviving my first winter in Alaska, and it made me feel even more welcomed. Eventually I found out it came from a coworker who wanted to share from the season's first catch.

Bethany Neubarth
Bethel

Size Matters

CHARLIE CAMPBELL

Charlie Campbell came to Alaska in 1975 and has commercially fished salmon in Kodiak and Bristol Bay. He currently lives in Tanana and runs a fishwheel on the Yukon River for king and chum salmon. As a regular columnist with the *Fairbanks Daily News-Miner* from 1989 to 2003, he wrote about Interior Alaska bush life, politics, and fisheries.

I'VE ATTENDED A LOT OF ALASKA BOARD OF FISHERIES MEETINGS over the years, but my gut told me today's meeting was going to be one of the worst. I felt I-told-you-so boiling up, but I told myself to control my anger and my nerves and be effective.

Fishing was over for the year, another in a series of dismal king salmon returns on the Yukon River. Now it was January 2013, and I had flown down to Anchorage from the village of Tanana to testify on behalf of our Tanana-Rampart-Manley Fish and Game Advisory Committee.

As I made my way into the meeting, already underway, I smelled crummy hotel coffee mixed with the familiar nervous sweat-scent of fishermen out of their comfort zone.

It had been about six years, but scanning the room it was interesting to see the same fishermen and managers from years back, a little grayer and a few pounds heavier in the same flannel shirts and suits. Nothing much had changed.

I looked for our upriver delegation and saw all three guys sitting together in the front row: Stan Zuray, like myself from Tanana; Virgil Umphenhour from Fairbanks; and Victor Lord from Nenana.

Across the aisle to the right were thirty or more fishermen from the Yukon Delta. Their main lobbyist was sitting right behind us, alongside one of the lower river managers from the Alaska Department of Fish and Game. Very cozy.

"Hey," I whispered, sliding into a seat next to Stan. "Are they taking testimony yet?"

"Not yet, just about to. We signed you up, and you're first."

On cue, the chairman began to speak. He was sitting in the center of the row of board members at a long table: they looked magisterial and forbidding.

"The first up is Charles Campbell. Please state who you are representing."

I thought, I bet they've never had a fisherman asking them to do anything quite like this.

I have to back up a bit here.

We have a beautiful subsistence and commercial fish camp in the middle of the Alaskan interior on the swift, wide Yukon River, plenty of deep water flowing through a cool verdant canyon among big granite boulders. We have a fishwheel and catch, cut, smoke, and dry king salmon and the good fall chum salmon for food. We cut the later poorer quality chums to feed our dog team through the winter.

This spot at the Rapids on the Yukon is the place Tanana people have always gathered to fish kings and chums. It's a cheerful, labor-intensive, cooperative endeavor with village friends and neighbors.

I came to this area around 1980 from Fairbanks (and before that New England and Ontario), looking for a life just like this. We raised our kids here at this fish camp and in Tanana, a mostly Athabascan village of 250 souls thirty-five miles away, a traditional trading area at the confluence of the Yukon and Tanana Rivers.

And what gorgeous kings! Even 730 miles from the mouth they are still robust and fat; it's still a long way to their spawning grounds.

Sometimes getting up in the morning to check the wheel and bring some fresh kings down to chill in a tank of cold running creek water with the day all sunny and new, I feel like the luckiest man in the world. The sound of a fishwheel splashing in the current is to me the very song of a hot summer day in the Interior. It makes me think of paradise, of what I have to lose.

Everybody raised in Tanana knows and values this life. If I run into someone there who can smell fish and cottonwood smoke on my clothes, they might say with satisfaction, "Mmm, you smell like camp! I'm hungry for fish, you got any?"

Then, about twelve years ago, the trouble began. We started noticing we weren't ducking so much in the smokehouse under the long cut strips that came from the biggest kings. The kings were . . . shrinking.

It's funny how fishermen are chronic optimists. You go up to the fish box on the wheel and you think, hey, there's a nice big king. The biggest in the last two weeks.

Then you weigh it, and find it's barely thirty pounds. Thirty-pounders used to be a twice-a-day occurrence. We'd catch several forty-pounders per week, and see a handful of fifty-pound-plus fish in the course of the season.

We haven't seen a fifty-pound king in ten years. We got one thirty-nine-pound king in 2013. The research project weighing and measuring our area's catch over the past ten years confirms this decline. In 2013 the average king sampled in our area weighed 13½ pounds! That's not what a king salmon used to be, that's what everybody called a jack.

Why does size matter? Because, the big females produce the most eggs, and the eggs are healthier and bigger. With their bulk and strength, the big kings can move large rocks out of the way to make their redds (nests) and are able to deposit those eggs deeper in the gravel, protection against predation. This expands their range on swift-running creeks—they can exploit locations where smaller fish can't.

The loss of the big kings is a classic symptom of selective overfishing. The consensus among many biologists is that the main culprit is overharvest with large mesh gillnets used for many years in the commercial fishery that selected out the biggest kings.

Drifting with gillnets was introduced to the commercial fishery in the lower river districts in the late 1970s, and by the mid-1980s, the catch numbers had ratcheted up dramatically. With 8½-inch mesh, the big females were getting hammered. Fred Anderson, an ADF&G Yukon River manager at the time notes that "the catch-per-unit effort went sky high." Only in 2010, after a decade of petitioning by upriver groups, did the board finally reduce the maximum mesh size to 7½ inches. Some have argued that this just targets the next age/size class down.

While anyone with gear in the water (including us) bears some responsibility, the lower river districts drift fishery caught most of these big fish.

It's not just size that's down, numbers are too. The U.S.-Canada Yukon Salmon Treaty Panel has set a minimum border passage escapement number of 42,500 kings. (Some argue the number is set too low.) In 2013 the joint U.S.-Canada sonar counting project near the village of Eagle counted 30,715 kings (including the little jacks) going into Canada. In fact, according to the sonar count, only two of the past seven seasons have produced border passage over the minimum!

A running fishwheel takes a simple grab-sample of whatever fish are going by rather than selecting for a certain size the way gillnets do. We saw a size decline that the gillnet fishermen could not—and we had been sounding the alarm for at least a dozen years. What was excruciating was that no one listened. Not the downriver fishermen, not the ADF&G, not the Board of Fisheries.

We upriver fishermen became increasingly shrill about the shrinking kings to any ADF&G person who would listen, at any meeting we attended; we got nothing back but skepticism and patronizing unconcern. Nobody wanted to admit that the run was failing on their watch.

Meanwhile, the big commercial interests in the Yukon Delta were in denial: the problem was ocean conditions . . . it was low water . . . it was high water . . . it was cyclical . . . it was imaginary.

Of course ADF&G's job on the Yukon is difficult: managing a mixed stock fishery destined for hundreds of tributaries in an opaquely silty river two thousand miles long. And if you make the wrong call, the fishermen howl. One could understand the habitual protective crouch.

But, considering that ADF&G's job is to make policy recommendations to the board, the department's passivity on the king decline was maddening. Why wouldn't they do something to save this fish stock?

Well, if ADF&G couldn't say it, we would.

"In summary, Mr. Chairman, our advisory committee is asking for a two-year moratorium on any kind of king salmon fishing or king bycatch in the entire Yukon River drainage, with a reassessment at the end of that two-year period. Thank you for your consideration."

The speech was over, but the board members' heads were all still up. And they had asked me questions—mostly about the problem of how kings could be released unharmed during a concurrent lower river commercial summer chum fishery.

After a few more fishermen testified, the chairman announced a short break. A board member walked up and said to me, "You know, while you were talking, the chairman passed me a note that said this was something we should seriously consider. Thank you for that testimony. Your AC has some courage."

At that point I began to feel hope for the first time in years that we on the Yukon might not repeat the depressing story of the king salmon on the Columbia River, or the cod in the Atlantic: going, going, gone.

But the board meeting went on for two more days. Plenty of time for testimony from the lower river about how important king salmon were to them and their ancestors, why they should be allowed a heavy commercial take of the summer chum salmon without worrying too much about king bycatch, how economically hard up they were, etcetera.

Meanwhile, the ADF&G people were busy keeping their heads down.

So, after all this, after the post-meeting lobbying in the hotel bar, after the long sit and the chance to reconsider, our fresh idea needed to be . . . adjusted downward a bit . . . moratorium was just a little too radical an idea for the moment.

About all the board did in the end was to mandate protecting the first pulse of kings with subsistence closures and to prohibit the sale of kings taken as bycatch during the lower river summer chum commercial fishery. Good, but small, tentative steps.

We didn't convince the Board of Fish or the lower river fishermen this time. But here you are reading this. And maybe you are even one of those folks. Here's what I say to you:

Get a backbone! Agree to a moratorium on the Yukon king salmon and on any king bycatch until they come back in strength. You can tell your grandkids that you did the right thing. Or you can tell them what a Yukon king used to look like.

My story goes back thirty years. I was four years old, fishing in Bird Creek with my father. I was so excited because I had my very own fishing pole! I stood on the bank and cast my line, hoping and wishing I'd get a bite. Suddenly I felt a tug that quickly turned into an intense struggle. I had a three-foot beautiful king salmon on my line! The fish pulled and fought as I reeled with everything in me. Needless to say, I lost the battle—and my fishing pole. But I gained something special that day, a love for fishing and my home state of Alaska.

Mi'chelle McCoy
Anchorage

I'm Yup'ik Alaskan and an avid fisherwoman for my family. I have been given the right tools and motivational support to pursue my heritage and live by our main diet—fish. Twenty-two years ago on my birthday, my great-grandparents gave me an *uluaq*, also known as an ulu or woman's knife. To this day I still own it, use it, and take care of it. It is very important to my family. The first summer after my birthday gift, I learned how to cut fish. There was an abundance of silvers and chums, which were cut and smoked, and the best kings were cut into long strips for food. My mother handed me my knife and told me to cut very carefully along a beautiful king full of firm meat. I have never forgotten who gave me these tools and am glad to have fishing in my life.

Adaline Pete
Stebbins

Here on the Rocks
SETH KANTNER

Seth Kantner is the author of *Shopping for Porcupine*, the novel *Ordinary Wolves*, and *Pup and Pokey*, an illustrated children's book. He recently released *Swallowed by the Great Land*. He lives with his wife and daughter in Northwest Alaska.

ALONG THE KOBUK RIVER, a few hundred yards from where I was born, a rock bar forms an ancient fishing eddy named Kapakavik. I boat out here often, or walk when the water is low. Now it's a gray evening, too warm for September, and wanting to rain. Underfoot the rocks are brown and uneven and polished. Each summer willows cover more and more of the bar. Along the edge, the current quickly becomes dark and deep, and I peer into it, wondering what the fish are doing down there in the relaxing depths.

Thinking about salmon, I smile at an irony that comes to mind—that similarity some of us share with these fish—an addiction to where we were born.

In local Inupiaq culture, I've noticed that people—when asked questions about who they are—almost always start by saying their parents' names, and where they themselves were born, and after that telling where they grew up.

Unknowingly, I guess I absorbed that way of considering myself. For decades I never realized why I do it; certainly it doesn't always fit into conversation in Fairbanks, Anchorage, and other cities. Somehow, here close to the land, we don't feel simply ourselves, but a combination of our parents and where we come from.

My family used to set nets off this shore for dog food and people food. Kapakavik in Inupiaq, we were told, meant "place where they spear salmon," but I have no idea how the people of the past did that, and my family never tried spearing anything.

The surface of the big river reflects the gray of the sky in approaching twilight, and a faint breeze carries along the stink of dead salmon. Down farther along the bar, young brown bear tracks meander the dark wet sand. Scattered here and there are dead salmon and other fish, washed ashore. Out in the main channel, the curved flank of a floating salmon spins slowly in the current.

This fall something is killing fish in the Kobuk River. None of the experts are quite sure yet why this is happening. The theory put forward is that our huge chum salmon run combined with unseasonably hot weather in August and no rain might have caused oxygen depletion in the water. An algae bloom, too, might have further reduced the level of oxygen in the river. So far no one knows for certain what has caused this strange loss of life.

On the rocks, I poke a stick into a gigantic sun-bleached fish, bloated like a hip boot full of oatmeal, nasty and reeking. I kneel down and peer into the hole I've twisted in the soft flesh. The rotten sperm sacks appear intact. I stroll to a smaller female, do the same, and discover orange eggs.

These salmon didn't spawn, and I don't believe the others along the shore did either. None of them have that spawned-out look I'd recognize. Glancing down the shore, from one to the next, I think about all this wasted food, and life, and I can't help fearing for our future. A feeling of loss comes over me, for these intense lives, lived with such force, and abandoned here, so close to completion.

Thinking about salmon—even out in the lonely Pacific—always brings me right back to Kapakavik, to this fishing eddy, and to my past. When I was young my parents needed a lot of protein for us and the dogs. My dad mostly shot caribou those first years, maybe fifty to one hundred caribou each autumn, because meat during the migration was handy on the hoof. When my family did finally acquire nets, we spent a lot of each fall fishing right here, drying countless fish for the winter.

Earlier, in 1960, my parents commercial fished for chum salmon in Kotzebue, for a floating cannery located there. The price was thirty-five cents a fish; boats and gear were rented from the cannery, and my mom always liked to report that they made only a hundred dollars that summer.

Later, in the spring of 1974, my dad and his close friend Keith Jones both built wooden boats near Ambler, and our families boated down the Kobuk, out to Kotzebue Sound to again commercial fish for salmon. This—the northernmost fishery in Alaska, virtually all chum salmon—was growing rapidly, and people were making money. Salmon fishing suddenly was a way for villagers to earn cash. Previously, the main ways for locals to make money were fur trapping and occasional summer construction jobs.

Living in leaky tents on the coast at Sisualik, we were damp a lot and worked hard. Soon there were bad years—poor returns—and fishermen railed at state biologists and blamed everything they could imagine, except themselves.

Back then, every weekend at the fish camp the fishermen listened to KOTZ AM radio for the openers. Fritz Coleman was the ADF&G biologist who announced his decisions. He cut us back in the mid-1970s from forty-eight-hour periods twice a week, to thirty-six hours, and finally to twenty-four-hour openers. Universally, folks hated him—which is why I remember his name today.

Most of us were from camps and villages, and we had long hours and days to sit in our wind-lashed tents, waiting, while fish passed, some jumping and the rest unseen under the waves. We had no iPhones, no four-wheelers, no video players, very little fresh water. We ate salmon every night unless a loon got in the net, or a porcupine wandered out the grassy spit. We fed flounders to our sled dogs, and we waited. We just wanted to FISH! And when the season ended, most of us packed our boats and went directly home up the Noatak and Kobuk Rivers, and to Kivalina, Deering, Buckland, Selawik, and camps in between—to fish more, for food. Because of the great numbers of fish we killed, we were sure we knew more about salmon than any Outsider biologist on the radio.

Slowly, over the years, from various biologists' excuses, reports, and reasoning, people learned a side of things we might not have known—bits and pieces, such as how the value of the Japanese yen affected our fish prices, how three-year-old salmon numbers predicted the following year's return, and five-year-olds could be counted on the year after a large run. We learned about roe maturity and quality, and fall rains washing out eggs, and spring floods flushing out fry. And words like "smolt," "escapement," "test-net," "sonar," and "aerial surveys."

Local fishermen were outraged to learn that False Pass boats in the Aleutians were intercepting *our* chums, as were Korean ships on the high seas with many-mile-long nets. Dips in fish prices didn't help the mood around Kotzebue Sound. The '80s had some good years, but on average our price kept falling, and in the '90s it rose briefly—then fell to pennies.

Meanwhile, more and more money poured into the region—in the form of hundreds of high-paying jobs, grants, machinery, handouts, low-income homes, free stove oil, etcetera. Salmon—as a career, a calling, a mainstay of life—largely receded into history. Only a few of us kept setting our nets, season after season, making less and less income from fish. And each year there were fewer dog teams; the ones that remained were mostly racing teams—huskies bred with hounds, the new dogs narrow, hyper, "crack-addict" racing dogs, pampered and often powered by imported chicken livers, beef, and New Zealand lamb.

Now, these last few years, our fishery is finally rebounding. The commercial salmon season this summer was a wild one; the run came early and continued in record numbers, and there were three buyers instead of the usual one. Without all three, we couldn't have handled the increase in boats, and so many fish. And the price rose—however briefly—to three times that of last season.

It was an alignment of the stars that our fishery hasn't enjoyed in a long time. Kotzebue felt again like it did back in the '70s—a fishing community, with fishermen moving with purpose on the shore, their sleeves stained and stinking and cash bulging in their pockets.

Meanwhile, this resurgence of our commercial salmon fishery is happening against the backdrop of fast-moving plans by the local Native corporation and Canadian mining conglomerates to build a road through to the headwaters of the Kobuk and pock the mountains north of the river with enormous open-pit mines.

Locally, the commonly held belief is that salmon will take care of themselves. The rhetoric put forth by proponents of this mega-project is that fish will be fine, unaffected by acid runoff; nothing will change and we can have our beautiful, perfect fish in our clean river *and* big new mines upstream. We can have it all.

This fall, the commercial salmon season has just wrapped up. Standing here on the rocks at Kapakavik, looking east, upstream toward where they want to build those mines and west down toward the coast—and looking back, too, over these decades of living along this river and commercial fishing these last forty summers—I realize an unholy number of salmon have passed through my hands. Especially when reflected against the amount of conservation effort, or anything else I ever put toward these amazing creatures. I've done nothing. I've simply loved fishing and fish and relied each year on them for both food and income.

These days melting permafrost due to climate change is draining thermokarst lakes on the nearby tundra. Warming is seeding the sandbars and hills and tundra with brush, tall alders, and trillions of new baby spruce. The rocks of the creeks feel different under my feet—slimy with algae—and from the sky I've photographed whole lakes now that are neon green.

Change is in the air, too, a climate of uncertainty—tangible in this unseasonably warm evening, the smell of greenery, the stink of rotting bodies—and somehow in our cells now, too, I'm beginning to believe. It's hard to know what to expect next.

Now, on the big river rain begins to patter down, splashing on the rocks around me. In the falling dusk I turn to walk across the bar and wade the shallows back to my home on the hill. Tonight I don't feel any of us have done anything spectacular here—only been lucky, inhabiting a spectacular place, at a spectacular time. One we've shared with salmon.

And when these silver companions of ours turn belly-up in midjourney and start floating dead down this pristine river, what else can we think but that somehow we are doing wrong, terribly wrong. We—none of us—have even begun the real work of doing right for these beautiful creatures, and for ourselves.

When I was about five years old, living in Seward, I went to the ferry dock where all the tourists were salmon fishing with their fancy new poles. I watched for a while, but nobody was catching anything. I climbed around the big rocks and found some discarded fishing line. I had a safety pin and tied that to the end of the line. Then I found a piece of driftwood and tied the other end of the line to it. The safety pin was too light and just floated on top of the water, so I pulled it in and tied a small rock to the line a short ways up from the pin and threw it back in the water.

It wasn't two minutes later when I felt a huge jerk on my little stick! I pulled, and it pulled back. Really, all I could do was hang on. I only weighed about forty pounds myself, so I had my knees braced against the breakwater, hanging on for dear life and thinking "Don't let it pull you in!"

That's when a nice gentleman came up with a net. My line was so short that the fish was fighting right on top of the water in front of me, and he easily dipped it out with his net. Everyone gawked with amazement as I hit its head with a rock and pulled the safety pin out of the big king's mouth. Some of them were mad at their own expensive rods, and I could hear them cussing.

The nice man who helped me asked if he could give me a ride to take it home. I didn't know him so I said no. I took a firm grip on the gills and proceeded to drag that poor fish right through the gravel all the way to Tony's Bar, where my mom worked. My mom and dad were so proud of me. We ate it for dinner that night.

Leona Gottschalk
Seward

Riversong

KIRSTEN DIXON

Kirsten Dixon has been living and cooking in the Alaska backcountry for more than thirty years. She divides her time between Winterlake Lodge, the Finger Lake checkpoint along the Iditarod Trail, and Tutka Bay Lodge in Kachemak Bay.

THE IDEA

When I got married, my husband, Carl, owned an Alaska river rafting company. He would return to our home in Anchorage from long trips and tell me stories about his adventures—the blueberries along the banks of a particular river, the fishing, or what food he cooked over the campfire in the evenings. One night, while we were dreaming out loud to each other, we made the decision to seek a life lived closer to nature. I wanted a garden with carrots that my babies could pull up from the ground, and Carl wanted to teach his children how to fish for salmon.

THE LODGE

In the fall of 1983, we climbed into a float-equipped Cessna 206 airplane: me, Carl, our little baby Carly, the dog, a broom and a mop, and boxes of food. The first snow had just begun to fall as we quietly glided onto the Yentna River, about forty-five minutes north of Anchorage by air. We had found a piece of land to buy. We were going to make our living by starting and running a sportfishing lodge.

We had to borrow a skiff to row across and downriver to the small two-room cabin that was our new home. The pungent smell of frosted lowbush cranberries forever reminds me of that first night on the river. Salmon carcasses, half buried and frozen in mud, were scattered along the riverbank, final remnants of the violence and the beauty of summer on the river.

In that first winter, Carl and I led the simple uncomplicated lives we had dreamed of. During the day, I kept the woodstove going and the baby fed while Carl worked on what would become the main building of the lodge we'd open the next summer. In the evenings, after the dishes were done, within the thick yellow glow of a kerosene lantern, we planned our new lives and our new lodge. We'd call it Riversong after a line from a Van Morrison song.

THE FISHING LIFE

Our lodge was located at the confluence of two rivers—the clear and cold waters of Lake Creek and the wide silty Yentna River. Large runs of salmon, all five species, returned to Lake Creek every year. In those early days, it was easy to attract fishermen to stay with us, given the lure of abundant sixty-plus-pound king salmon that swam in the river right out our front door. The news of the first salmon caught in the springtime always spread up and down the river with breathless urgency, by boat or CB. Those of us, just a few families living along the eighteen-mile stretch of river between Lake Creek and Skwentna, were first witnesses to the miracle of salmon leaping out of the water once again. The news somehow bound us together in collective appreciation for the salmon returning. When the biggest fish were in, king salmon that weighed nearly more than I could lift, the energy on the river was palpable.

Our little lodge grew, cabin by cabin. Each winter, Carl worked on a new building project and I learned how to cook for our guests. Fishermen came to stay with us from every corner of the world. At night, our little bar would be packed with convivial fishermen telling stories of their lives at home, of their faraway families, and the adventures of the day. The lodge hummed with the brightness of happy people. In the fall, all the people would go away. And so would the bears and the birds, each of us depending on the salmon to return the next season. Salmon eggs, salmon fry, salmon flesh, and salmon carcasses had fed us all. The salmon in the river gave us our livelihood, our lives together. The salmon in the river had fed us, spiritually as well as literally. Sometimes I wore little dangling preserved salmon-eye earrings.

And every summer the fish came back. Our daughters learned to fish. They could spin-cast and fly-cast. They held beating bloody salmon hearts in their hands. They drove boats as well as any fishing guide. Catches were hung onto hooks underneath a sign my mother painted and pictures were taken with grinning proud people. I grilled and broiled, fried, and steamed salmon. We had big barbecues on our deck with bluegrass music playing.

WHERE DID THE SALMON GO?

I'm not quite sure when our lives began to change at Riversong. Perhaps it was with the first airboat arrival from downriver, pulsing a deafening winded sound across the garden. Maybe it was gunshots in the night announcing a new neighbor's inebriated expression of freedom and signaling the end of our own. Maybe it was when guests began to come back to the lodge without fish. No one knew why our fish weren't returning. In those years, we never considered that the salmon wouldn't return. I suppose we had thought that our lives, just as they were, would go on forever. There were grumbles and whispers at our dinner table where the fishing guides gathered. The fish had been, perhaps, intercepted in the ocean by commercial fishermen or overfished by sport fishermen. The fish returns were half of what they were when we first moved to Lake Creek. Every season ended with optimism that the next year's run would be better.

Despite the decline, people kept coming to our river to catch salmon. Airplanes filled to capacity with day-fishers from Anchorage kept launching from Lake Hood like miniature squadrons off to war. Airplanes circled overhead of our idyllic homestead with such velocity, at times I couldn't hear anything but the drone and throttle-down of engines. Fishermen came from cruise ships and packaged tours, wanting to catch an Alaska fish on the quick and easy. "Let's Go Fishing" blasted over the Anchorage airwaves. Arctic terns circled and cried, competing for the gravel bar that had been their nesting ground but was now a busy floatplane parking lot.

SAYING GOODBYE

After more than twenty years of living at Lake Creek, Carl and I decided to leave our beloved lodge. The changes to the river and the changes to us left too much uncommon ground. We had never meant our little lodge to grow so big. We never meant to catch so many fish. There were now a dozen or so wilderness lodges lining the banks of the river. We moved farther west and north of Lake Creek to start a new lodge, higher into the valley and closer to the mountains, but far enough away for me to long for those tall swaying cottonwood trees along the riverbanks.

We still fish for salmon in the small streams that surround us and on a few lakes nearby. But I never see Arctic terns anymore and I miss that annual river-wide announcement that the king salmon have returned.

Riversong has survived beyond us. I've heard through the grapevine a new family lives there. I hope they'll take good care of the lodge, and the river. I hope they'll plant a garden and respect the fragility of the balance of it all.

POSTSCRIPT: FIRST SALMON

Gill and gut your first king salmon of the season. Wash it well with clean, cold water and pat it completely dry. Fillet both sides with a sharp ten-inch breaker knife. Use a spoon to scrape the remaining meat off of the carcass. (You'll get nearly a pound more of meat by doing this. It can go into the spaghetti sauce the next day.) Pull out all thirty-two pin bones from both fillets with a flat-edged Japanese fish tweezer, being careful not to tear the flesh. Season both sides with salt and pepper. Rub both sides with good quality olive oil. Brush the flesh with lime juice, honey, and ginger. Grill the salmon skin-side down over hot alder wood, covering the lid so the smoke stays in. Cook for about eight minutes per inch of flesh, just until the fat begins to release. Be thoughtful to whom you give the first serving—it's good luck that will last the entire summer.

It was a sunny eighty degrees on the Talkeetna River. We had three poles rigged and in the water. After a few nibbles, one rod began to bob violently. I released it from the holder and handed it to Ellie, our three-year-old. She squealed with glee the entire time she reeled in the fish. When Daddy got the silver salmon up onto the bank, Ellie's grin was ear to ear. She laughed and hugged the giant fish to her chest as she posed for her photograph—her very first salmon! That night, as she devoured her portion, she exclaimed, "Mommy, this is delicious! We should get more!" Another die-hard fishergirl was born!

Jenny Fast
Anchorage

My earliest salmon memory starts with a simple line tied to a stick, fishing for kings in the Little Su. I remember looking across the water and thinking I could run across the backs of the fish to the other side.

Danika Simpson
Anchorage

Bristol Bay Youth Doing Their Part

VERNER WILSON III

Verner Wilson III was born and raised in Dillingham. As a Bristol Bay salmon fisherman his entire life, he's been inspired to be active in the region's pressing environmental issues and to help protect his Yup'ik Eskimo cultural traditions. He received a degree in environmental studies from Brown University in 2008 and a master's in environmental management from Yale University in 2015.

EVERY SUMMER, AFTER SCHOOL WAS OUT, MY FRIENDS AND I PREPARED. The trees and plants flourished, the days grew long. Excitement was in the air and all around. We knew life was coming back to our region, in all shapes and sizes. Whether a bear or a fox coming out of its den, an eagle building a nest, a beluga whale splashing around, or one of thousands of fishermen, we all awaited one thing: the return of a keystone fish.

This is the magic that the young people of Bristol Bay witness year after year: millions of sockeye salmon bringing us together. We mend nets, get all of the equipment and supplies ready. The beginning of summer is a time of family, friends, and fish camp; of sharing, community, hard work, and great reward. Freezers fill for the winter; money is earned. Our Yup'ik, Aleut, Dena'ina, and other cultural traditions are fulfilled with our family and fish camp friends.

One of my first memories was when I was around five years old at fish camp in Clark's Point of Nushagak Bay. I pulled a salmon from our set-net and tried to save it by throwing it back in the water, but my grandma stopped me. She said, this is our food and our way of life. This is how we survive year after year and how our ancestors fed their children in a tradition that has continued for thousands of years.

During my young years, I didn't know that where we came from had the largest wild sockeye salmon fishery in the world. Thousands of fish caught in our nets during a summer day was normal to me. But after I learned, I was thankful. Thankful not just for the resources it gives to us, the healthy nourishment and hard-earned cash, but for the time spent with my parents, grandma, siblings, aunts, uncles, and friends. I really got to know my dad and brother while on the boat. From them I learned the value of teamwork and the virtues of patience and determination. Fishing also gave me childhood friends and memories that can never be taken away.

After working hard on the boats and the beach, toward the end of the summer we would travel up to the beautiful freshwater lakes that dot the Bristol Bay region. The spawning salmon swam about under the crisp clear water, along with pike, trout, Dolly Varden, and other prized fish. In my second-ever cast of a sportfishing rod, I caught a prized rainbow trout. I remember my dad being so proud.

Growing up, we thought our commercial, subsistence, and sport fisheries, and everything that came with them, could never be taken away from us. Or so we thought.

In 2004 my friends and I learned of a potentially large gold and copper prospect nearby. Many people thought that this was an additional resource blessing; the mine could be worth billions of dollars and bring full-time jobs. Little did we know the proposed Pebble Mine would turn into a test for us.

Our elders did a lot of work for all of us to understand what a major mine in the region meant. We heard from the mining company and from biologists, geologists, and other experts in different fields. The more we heard of the Pebble prospect, though, the more concerned we became for our most valued treasures—our clean water and our red gold. Large-scale mines inevitably pollute.

We learned of other parts of the world. How they used to have huge salmon runs that are now diminished and gone. Even my grandpa traveled across the world to follow the fish, from Finland to Astoria, Oregon, to Alaska. Habitat degradation and poor management practices decimated fisheries across Europe, along the East Coast of North America, through the Pacific Northwest.

The more we learned about Pebble, the more it became unacceptable to us. The elders taught us youth to cherish our traditions and to keep them alive. My friends and I felt that it was up to us to make sure our culture and livelihoods were passed on for the future. Perhaps that is why the youth have been some of the most ardent opponents of Pebble and any industrial mining district in Bristol Bay. We see our future and our people at stake.

This danger to our fishery has awoken a young giant. When we first heard about the proposed mine a decade ago as college students spread across the country, a group of us immediately organized via phone. We asked what we could do to understand the issue and to make sure our voices were heard. Our desire to influence our future has encouraged many of us to dedicate our lives to the protection of our fishery. For me personally, I feel like I would not be able to live with myself if I wasn't involved for the protection of our salmon. I know that is how many of my peers feel.

As a result, the younger generations of Bristol Bay have become activists. Young people have already run for office and have won leadership posts on the platform to protect our way of life. Middle and high school students have led pep rallies, marches, and demonstrations to protect Bristol Bay. They even organized a group called Rebels to Pebble. One of my dear friends, Apayo Moore, has been using her passion to protect our fishery through the creation of beautiful salmon art, inspiring everyone so much that she won the Bristol Bay Native Corporation's Citizen of the Year award. Others are creating beautiful salmon clothing and regalia that are worn by young people across the region. Some are dedicating their lives to conservation by going to college and getting degrees for sustainable careers—their educations funded by commercial fishing. Others are passing on the tradition of fishing, taking over boats and permits themselves in their teens and early twenties to start their own businesses. A few are doing a combination of fishing in the summer and campaigning to protect Bristol Bay in the winter.

I am proud to say that I am a member of the younger generation of Bristol Bay that is passionate, motivated, and dedicated.

Our youth-led movement has even grown around the state. Youth from villages and towns across coastal Alaska have been signing petitions and taking action. Protecting our salmon was recently the campaign of choice by Alaska Youth for Environmental Action, which has chapters and thousands of members across the state. It's inspiring to see the future leaders of Alaska stepping up for our wild salmon.

In my former job at the World Wildlife Fund, I traveled across the nation to get our message across. I talked with people from Dutch Harbor to New Stuyahok, from Seattle to Washington, D.C. While striving for my master's degree in environmental management at Yale University, I continued to tell our story. When people ask where I'm from, I tell them amazing facts about Bristol Bay. I tell them of the strength of the king salmon run in the Nushagak River. I tell them our wild salmon fed America's victorious army during World War II. I tell them of the healthy omega-3 fatty acids that are good for their hearts. I tell them that nearly half of all wild sockeye salmon in the world come from my region. I tell them of the thousands of young people from across America who depend on the region's fisheries to get through college themselves.

During my work, I was even able to discuss these facts with influential people like former secretary of the interior Ken Salazar when he visited Dillingham in 2009. After the trip, the secretary proclaimed that "Bristol Bay is a national treasure that we must protect for future generations" before placing protections against offshore drilling there. I also talked with hundreds of staffers in the legislature and Congress about why protecting the region is important. I am just one young person from Bristol Bay who has gotten over fears of public speaking to tell our story. Our hard work has made a difference. Our leaders are listening and taking steps to protect Bristol Bay.

The year 2014 was especially good for the protection of my home region due to the great work of the many people dedicated to our cause. The Obama Administration, through the Environmental Protection Agency, concluded three years of its scientific homework regarding the mine in January. The agency's study underwent two drafts after receiving extensive advice from more than a million public comments and two reviews by an independent panel of environmental experts. Less than two months after releasing its findings, EPA took bold steps by proposing commonsense restrictions to protect Bristol Bay's wild salmon resource from the adverse environment effects of mining the Pebble deposit. When announcing the protections, EPA administrator Gina McCarthy proclaimed, "This 404(c) process is not something, and I want to stress this, that the agency does very often, but the Bristol Bay fishery is an extraordinary resource and it's worthy of out-of-the-ordinary agency actions to protect it." (Unfortunately, the EPA's authority was challenged, and multiple lawsuits by Pebble proponents have slowed protections.)

Alaskans had their own say on the matter during the November 2014 general election. A state ballot measure called Bristol Bay Forever asked Alaskans if they wanted another layer of state protection for the region after decades of controversy. By nearly two to one, Alaskans voted to require a scientific finding to prove a large-scale metallic sulfide mine like Pebble would not endanger the fishery. This new law also requires legislative approval for such a mine.

And then, at year's end, President Obama acted to permanently protect the offshore areas of Bristol Bay from oil and gas drilling. This is an important acknowledgment of the region's incredible salmon resource and economy.

The region now enjoys federal and state protections to deter destructive development. It has been inspiring to work with my peers to make such a difference. I know that moving forward, we will teach the young leaders of tomorrow to carry the torch. Bristol Bay's rich fisheries can be here for thousands of years more if they continue the efforts to take care of them. The youth of the future have the tools to protect the world's greatest wild salmon runs.

You stand shoulder to shoulder at the mouth of the Kenai River, with your five-foot net attached to a ten-foot pole. You feel crazy alive. You wait for a sockeye salmon to swim into your net. Not the net inches from yours. Not the net at the front of the line. But yours. You wait. And you wait. You talk to the people around you, as diverse as they come. You are all the same. Waders and nets.

You stare at the light on the water, the volcanoes in the distance: Redoubt, Spurr, Iliamna, St. Augustine. You observe the various people down the line: Alaska Native, Samoan, Hmong, old and young, all waiting with a net similar to yours. You turn and watch the action on the beach, the tribe that comes together every second or third week in July.

You promise to say thank you before you kill, grateful. Mmm, salmon. Salmon fillets, salmon cakes, salmon burgers, salmon tacos, salmon quesadillas, smoked salmon, salmon pesto pasta, salmon scrambled eggs, salmon salad, salmon lasagna, jarred salmon, salmon sandwiches, salmon jerky, salmon quiche: you name it, you'll eat it, all winter long. It's one of the many reasons you love Alaska.

And when you finally catch a fish, you cheer and dance around the net. Thank you, you tell the salmon, thank you. You lay your hands on silver scales and study your first fish of the season longer than normal after waiting so long. Thank you, thank you, you repeat, before raising your wooden bonker and hitting it twice on the head. You slit the gills with your bare hands, using your forefinger as a knife, and then carry this gift to the ocean's edge to clean off the sand and silt. You hold the sockeye that found your net amidst the rest high above your head and smile at your family and friends who wave and cheer from the campsite. You smile from every fiber that makes you alive. Then you turn and walk back into the water, wielding your giant net like a direct line between family and sea, and you silently thank your own version of god for this rich, salty life of yours.

Christy Everett
Anchorage

In Cook Inlet, commercial setnetters work short anchored gillnets from skiffs. Competition among user groups has made management of the "mixed stock" Cook Inlet fisheries difficult and has resulted in reduced fishing periods.

(Top): The annual Bristol Bay Salmon Camp is held on the shores of Lake Aleknagik. In an intensive science course, high school students learn about the natural history of salmon, the region's ecosystems, sustainability, and field research methods.

(Top left): Setnetting is a way of life for 736 Cook Inlet commercial permit holders and often involves entire families. Eighty-four percent of permit holders are Alaskans, with most of those living on the Kenai Peninsula.

(Bottom left): The setnet fishery in Bristol Bay catches, on average, 12 percent of the total Bristol Bay catch. When the tide goes out, picking nets can be muddy, back-breaking work.

(Top): At a culture camp conducted by the Calista Heritage Foundation in southwest Alaska, students learn traditional practices from elders and work together in subsistence activities, including catching and preparing salmon.

(Top left): Dipnetting for sockeye salmon at the mouth of the Kenai River is a very popular personal-use fishery. Every July Alaskans harvest up to a half million sockeye salmon for their own use. The personal-use catch limits for upper Cook Inlet are twenty-five salmon for each permit holder and another ten for each additional member of the household.

(Bottom left): Drift gillnetting, here near Sand Point in southwest Alaska, is not to be confused with large-scale pelagic drift-net fishing, which was banned in international waters in 1992. Salmon fishing has a very low incidence of bycatch.

Recipes and methods for drying and smoking salmon differ widely between regions and families. Smoking is common in parts of the state where wood, often alder, is in good supply, while in drier, windier, treeless regions salmon are often air dried.

The Gold Creek Salmon Bake in Juneau has been operating for thirty seven years as an outdoor, all-you-can-eat, all-summer-long event.

At the Bristol Bay Fly Fishing Guide Academy, young Alaskans learn the art of fly fishing and explore careers as guides. The academy was begun as a way to encourage locals to enter the guiding workforce, where they can earn a living while protecting their heritage lands and waters and providing visitors with a richly Alaskan experience.

Let Nothing Be Wasted

LESLIE LEYLAND FIELDS

Leslie Leyland Fields is the author of nine books including *Surviving the Island of Grace* and *The Spirit of Food*. She spends most of her life on two islands, Kodiak Island in the winter and Harvester Island in the summer. She works with her family in commercial salmon fishing and spends as much time as possible making her favorite food—smoked salmon.

IT WAS ALASKAN SALMON that got me into Michel's boat on the Sea of Galilee last November. It was a windy morning, the waters chopping into flecks of white. The boardwalk was empty, except for a father and a son flying a kite. I scanned the main dock, which harbored three of the Holy Land boats and a handful of smaller dinghies and sport boats, all that was left in the water for the winter season. I was about to give up my quest to go out with a fisherman, disappointed, when I saw a man sitting on the steps in boots. Knee boots. The kind fishermen might wear. I took a deep breath and neared the dock gate. His back was facing me.

"Excuse me, do you speak English?" I ventured.

He turned to look at me. "Yah, a leetle." He was completely bald, with a brown face and heavy black eyebrows. He looked at me with curiosity.

"Are you a fisherman?"

"Yah, I'm a fisherman," he nodded.

"Me, too," I said. "I'm from Alaska. We fish for salmon. Do you know salmon?"

"Alaska! Salmone!" He nearly jumped to his feet at the name of the fish. I couldn't help smiling. He pronounced it like the French do, sounding the *l* and making the *o* a long vowel. He faced me now, the dock gate between us. "Yes, I see on TV show. Beeg fish!" And he opened his arms about two feet.

"Yes!" I nodded back, laughing.

"You? Fisherman?" He was puzzled.

"Yes, sometimes. And all of my family—all fishermen. Look, I have some video. I show you!" I had not planned this, but I remembered that I had two videos from fishing still on my phone.

He opened the gate from inside and stepped out onto the concrete boardwalk, standing just a foot away from me now. I pulled out the phone, found the videos, and played the first one. We're on the ocean in a skiff. Suddenly an enormous fin whale surfaces just a few feet from our skiff, blasting air and sea through its cavernous blowhole.

"Whoa! What fish . . . ahhhhh . . ." He searched for the word.

"Whale. It's a fin whale."

"Fin whale," he repeated.

"Here, let me play it again."

The fisherman laughed this time, shaking his head. I guessed he was about my age, maybe closer to sixty.

"Here's another one." I played the next, which was video shot out in a big storm, blowing thirty-five knots, the water peeled to white, the skiffs pitching madly, the nets straining, all the fishermen encased in orange raingear, hoods over faces, like wraiths as they pull in the salmon.

"Oohhhh, big storm," he said, whistling under his breath. Then "sal-mone!" as he recognized the fish pulled in from the frothing waters. A man started to pass us while we were watching. The fisherman called to him, and he came over to watch with us. I played it again.

When it was over, the fisherman spoke to the other in Hebrew. I heard "Alaska" and "sal-mone" again while they both looked at me with interest.

I hoped I'd established my credentials. I was ready to go further. "What do you fish for here?"

"Everything. I fish everything here: muscht, biny, carp." He waved his hand.

"Where is your boat?"

"There." He pointed to a small wooden dinghy painted blue at the end of the dock. I saw his net in the boat, a clear monofilament. This passes no kind of muster in Alaska, neither the net nor the boat, but I tried not to judge or be disappointed by anything.

This was my fourth time to Israel, but it had been thirty years since my last. I know I went out on the Sea of Galilee on a tour boat in previous visits, but I had little recollection of it. Visually, there is little that is remarkable about the lake. It's small, just sixty-five square miles, and the mountains surrounding it are bland and mostly featureless. Once you've fished on the open ocean in Alaska, at the foot of mountain ranges, you're harder to impress. But it is the lowest lake in the world, sitting an astonishing 686 feet below sea level. And it feeds the Jordan River, the site of some of Israel's most defining moments in history.

I was there this time for research for a book, exploring the connections between water, fish, and holiness in the gospels and in my own life on Alaskan waters.

"When do you go out?" I hoped I was not being too pushy, but I had only four days left in Israel.

"At night. In the morning." He was noncommittal. "Now it's too windy. Too much waves. I'm waiting if the wind comes down," he said, looking out at the water.

We talked for thirty more minutes. His name was Michel. He'd been fishing on the lake since he was fifteen. There were forty other small boats that worked these inland waters, supporting about a hundred people, he told me. And there was only one bigger boat, a seine boat, still allowed to fish. Three seiners used to work these waters, but they fished too well. There are not so many fish as there used to be, Michel informed me. He spoke without emotion or concern. I wanted to know more, but he was impatient with my questions.

"When the wind comes down and you go out, I can go out with you?" I asked.

"Yah, Yah!" he waved his hand dismissively, like we'd gone over this a hundred times.

We went out the next night. It was nearly 5:00 p.m. and dark. I stepped into the boat cautiously, feeling like I was going to tip it over. It was so small, and the sides came up just to my knees. Was there really room for me? Michel took his place in the stern, beside the fifteen-horse outboard, and Mickey, his crewman, sat near him. I sat in the bow. Michel pulled the engine to life and we rumbled out of the tiny harbor in the dark.

My expectations were high, but Michel was low key. It was near the end of the muscht season, he told me. The lake levels were low, but the price was good. Muscht was the Hebrew name for tilapia, also known as St. Peter's fish. Michel sold mostly to the restaurants on the promenade. The tourist season was waning as Christmas neared, but still, nearly every tourist who comes to the Sea of Galilee will have a dinner of this St. Peter's fish, named after the disciple who caught a fish with a coin in its mouth to pay a tax.

We were out for several hours—setting the nets imported from Japan, with detergent bottles for buoys. The nets were much smaller than ours, the mesh openings tighter. They were lighter as well, just monofilament, where ours are multistrand, heavier for heavier fish, for strong tides and hard weather. Despite all my anticipation, the night was disappointing. After setting both long nets, letting them soak, pulling them in, in all that expanse, through all that water, two tiny fish appeared, neither sellable. We fished half the night—and caught nothing.

Early the next morning, we went out again, just at sunrise. We motored along the shoreline in the rosy haze of the early sun. An egret landed two feet from me in the bow and stayed with us. We passed a row of first-class hotels just as the smell of sewage hit my nose. I glanced at Michel to see if he registered the foul smell at all. He did not. But I knew its source: I had read before I came that the hotels dumped their untreated sewage straight into the lake. To my surprise, Michel chose this very area to set his net. Later that day, I watched him pour water from a jug into a plastic cup. He drank it, then tossed the cup overboard along with the cellophane wrapper from the box of cookies they ate for lunch. Garbage came in with each pull of the net.

I understand why people mistake the ocean as a limitless resource that can absorb every offense in its incalculable vastness. But this lake, this "sea" I can encompass in a single glance? Who could miss its fragility, its limits? And this body of water is considered sacred, holy to many around the world. Nearly three million people will visit its shores each year, venerating the waters Jesus lived beside, that he walked upon, that he calmed with a command, "Peace! Be still!" These holy waters also collect the agricultural runoff from the hillsides around its shores, runoff that has turned the Jordan River into a thickened greenish soup, barely moving.

Michel didn't catch much that day either. In fact, fishermen rarely catch many fish anymore. Before 2005, 295 tons of St. Peter's fish were caught annually. In 2009, the total was only 8 tons. In 2010, stocks had fallen so low fishing was banned entirely for two years.

It is hard to make sense of this blindness and abuse here on the very lake where Jesus spread the good news of the coming of the Lord, where fish were multiplied and miraculous catches broke fishing nets. Abundance has been the rule for centuries in this lake. The nineteenth-century English clergyman Henry Baker Tristram recorded that "the density of the shoals of fish in the Sea of Galilee can scarcely be conceived by those who have not witnessed them." And now—the fish are few. Holy waters will not absorb and absolve our sin and our guilt. The plastic will not degrade. The fish will not multiply. The water will only dirty us; it will not cleanse. Why do we close our eyes and kill what we need, even what we venerate?

I have a guess. I know what happens in abundance, when fish fill your nets, sinking under their weight. When the boats are so laden with silver, they threaten to swamp. In my early years of fishing off Kodiak Island, in the late 1970s, salmon overwhelmed us for weeks. Again in 2005 and 2006—years we call "Humpy Hell"—our fishing nets were sunk with pink salmon. I watched my children pull fish from the nets until they could no longer stand. I watched my husband thrash his arms in sleep, arms gone numb with carpel tunnel. The fish filled the totes, some spilled over, some fell out of the nets. We did not care. They weren't worth much. There were so many fish the canneries were paying us only five cents a pound. A skiff full of fish made us each less than a hundred dollars. They lost their shine, these salmon, beautiful any other time. But when fish are thick, when anything we love and need is plentiful, something dies. We forget to look. We do not see their beauty, their scales like armor, fit each to each, their silver-stippled sides, their shimmering backs, their blue eyes, their rainbow tails. Even as we hold them in our cramping hands, then toss them into totes of ice, they are lost to us. We waste them. We cannot see beyond the moment. We imagine they are inexhaustible, these fish. These waters. We believe they are all here for us. We cannot imagine a river drying up, a drought of salmon, an emptied lake. We do not know we are that powerful, that wrong. We don't know it starts with closing our eyes.

This is our human history. We are inclined to waste, all of us.

We cannot *not* create waste. Even the purest water will turn to waste in our bodies. There is always something left over. Only the dead produce nothing. But we're wasteful in our waste. In America, we generate 250 million tons of waste annually. We bury more than 30 million tons of food in landfills every year. We throw too much away because we buy too much. And we buy too much because, in the land of plenty, we don't know the difference between need and want. It is clear: in our all-too-human economy, the more we have, the more we squander.

While pulling those empty nets on the lake in Galilee, I knew I was just a few miles from the hillside where another economy had been displayed. The gospels tell us that two thousand years ago more than five thousand people gathered to hear the words of a strange rabbi. When he stopped teaching, when it was time to eat, there was no food but one boy's sack lunch of five barley loaves and two small fish. How could so little feed such a hungry throng? Jesus broke the bread and the fish, thanked God, and passed them from hand to hand, somehow the fish and bread splitting, multiplying to fill every mouth, every appetite. When all had eaten, astonished at the bounty, He was not done. Jesus rounded his disciples and instructed them, "Gather the pieces that are left over. Let nothing be wasted."

They must have protested. What was the sense of this? When food is sparse, when resources are thin, when a god is limited and his miracles cautious and rare, we expect frugality. *Yes, save every crust! Who knows when more is coming!* But when the God of all plenitude has just filled every appetite and need—and can do it again and again? Even then, *Let nothing be wasted?* Yes, even then. Especially then. In times of bounty as well as in times of want, God's resources never lose their value.

It has always been so, since the very beginning, since the first "Let there be" was spoken out of the mouth of the Creator God. Can we envision the flocks of birds, the hordes of animals, the masses of fish sent spinning and swimming in those new seas? And then, into all this thriving world, came Adam, *Adam*, formed from the dirt, the Hebrew word *adamah*, which tells us something crucial about man and his place in creation. *Adamah* is not simply ground or dirt, but specifically "arable soil." The soil-man, who bears as well "the image of God," is placed in a place that further locates and identifies him: "The Lord God took the man and put him in the Garden of Eden to cultivate it and watch it." To cultivate and watch it, guard it.

That task is extended beyond the garden to all of creation and its creatures when God commands the first man and woman to "fill the earth and subdue it. Rule over the fish of the sea and the birds of the air and over every living creature that moves on the ground." Man and woman, then, are given a specific task and position: to act as God's representatives over all that was made, to bring it under God's authority that it might multiply and flourish. Multiply and flourish.

Here is the truth that matters to all of us. We don't own creation. Even when we hold a deed to a piece of land, or a license to fish a piece of water, we are caretakers who must not exploit or destroy at the pleasure of our own will. We will not regain our proper footing in this world—or the next—until we recover our identity as people of the soil and water, who live and work in right relationship to God and his creation.

But even within the gates of the garden, all is not this simple. The creation account contains a tension between the essential humility of humans, made from "humus," the earth, but who are then given the authority to "rule and subdue" all the other creatures, also made of humus. But we must get this balance right. When we focus more on our authority rather than our responsibilities in creation, nature may be seen as existing solely for our own purposes and pleasures, setting the stage for environmental exploitation. Lynn White made just such a charge in his 1967 watershed essay, "The Historical Roots of Our Ecological Crisis." White attacked Christianity as "the most anthropocentric religion the world has seen." He characterized the Christian perspective as the belief that "nature has no reason for existence save to serve [humans]." Thus, for White, Christian arrogance toward nature "bears a huge burden of guilt" for the contemporary environmental crisis.

I cannot deny some truth in these charges. But a growing number of eco-theologians are opening our eyes and righting the balance, offering biblical support for a humbler view of humankind as a member in a "community of creation" rather than a lord over it. Adam and Eve were introduced to a world already buzzing and humming and teeming with creatures who were blessed before we people even showed up. Yes, man and woman are uniquely made in the image of God, the *imago Dei,* and are given rule over creation, but they are to use and cultivate the earth in such a way that the birds of the air, the fish, and all creeping things, whom God delights in and pronounces "very good"—the same words used for humans—can likewise feed, multiply, and flourish. That all creatures may feed, multiply, and flourish. This is how our own presence blesses all of creation. We are here for this: to bless.

How do I say this to Michel? We are two people who love fish and water, and for these hours, we share a tiny boat on a small sea, but language comes between us. I don't know how to make him see the trash he throws in the water. I don't know how to ask him why he sets his net in the hotel sewage. I don't know what he believes in, and it's too hard for me to ask.

I know that when I return to Alaska, the salmon season will soon be upon us. My thirty-eighth season. As I fly out to our fish camp with my family I know the salmon will return as well. For now. I'm grateful for the biologists at the Alaska Department of Fish and Game who regulate our fisheries so well. Most of Alaska's salmon stocks are immense. But I know our human heart. I know how easy it is to stop watching, to cut the research and management funds, to open a mine that would drain toxins into our waters. I know our ocean is acidifying at alarming rates. I know we've believed too long this earthly garden is ours to exploit and exhume.

Our task now is the same as the moment we were made: to cultivate and watch. We will guard the purity of our waters. We will pull plastic from the waters and tide lines. When I go out to the nets to pick salmon from the ocean, I'll gaze at them again. I'll hold a red salmon in my hands and feel its weight, admire its fit of scale on scale. I'll wonder at the abundance of the pink salmon that sometimes fill our nets in miraculous proportions—each, still, a gift from a generous God. I'll place my hand on the rainbow fan of a king salmon tail, marveling. When I walk a salmon in each hand up to my house, to the kitchen, I will carve every bit of flesh from its bones. From our salmon dinners, I will toss what's left into chowder. I will fillet the silvers and pinks carefully, packing them neatly into the freezer for the winter ahead. Every bite will taste of ocean and care. Every bite will feed and nourish my family and friends and all who gather for potlucks at our church and our house. And look how filled we are! Let there be and there was . . . and it was good, very good. Let nothing be wasted. Not this ocean, not any lake or sea, not a single fish. Let the hungry gather. Let us offer what we have—two small fish that we raise our heads and thank God for, then break and pass from hand to hand to hungry mouth until all are filled, and still we pass the basket, collecting now what's left for any more who hunger and need. *Let nothing be wasted.* Like this, *Let nothing be wasted.*

I started commercial fishing when I was six. I know that sounds far-fetched, but my job was to put the outboard into reverse and guide the boat across the Kuskokwim River as my dad set the fifty-fathom drift net. When I was twelve, he put a limited entry commercial fishing permit in my name, and I was officially the captain. By fourteen there were the rare occasions I had to fish alone if my crew didn't show up.

In 1986 my family started tendering. We would ice up the boats and get the cash box, drive upriver, and wait for the deliveries. My dad ran the scale, I pitched fish, and my sister handled the fish tickets and cash box. In 1988 we had a banner year. I took full advantage of it by commercial fishing during the openers and then pitching fish after the openers for my dad's tender and the processor back in Bethel.

I assumed back then that my future children and grandchildren would also grow up in a commercial fishing family. The fishing industry has changed, though, and the Kuskokwim is no exception. Kusko commercial fishing is a shadow of its former self. Now even subsistence fishing is not guaranteed. We've depended on that annual process of harvesting (dried and smoked, pressure cooked and frozen) salmon not just for our larders but as a way to actively express our identity as people who live off the land and water.

This year my family members were active participants and supporters of the chinook conservation effort. It has been emotional to see our runs reduced to this. The restrictions have brought out the worst in some people. The assignment of blame and lack of willingness to problem solve has been draining.

I'm thankful for and enjoy the reds, chums, and cohos I'm able to catch and put up for the winter. I pray that our kings return in abundance. Not for me, or for commercial fishing, but for all of our descendants and the ecosystem that depends on them.

Mary Sattler
Bethel

The One That Got Away

DON REARDEN

Don Rearden is the author of the novel *The Raven's Gift*. He lives in Anchorage and is an associate professor at the University of Alaska Anchorage.

I STOOD AT THE BOW OF THE EIGHTEEN-FOOT LUND and fed out the net as my dad steered the boat backward against the current. The long string of white floats, nylon netting, and lead-weighted line played out in a forty-foot arc across the river, with each of the oval floats thumping against the aluminum as they popped over the rim of the boat's bow and splashed into the churning, murky water of the Kuskokwim.

My teenage mind drifted with the current as I tried to imagine how a Yup'ik fisherman, on that same stretch of river in the time of skin boats, would have secured a sinew-woven net against the riverbank, pushed off from the shore, and dipped the double blades of his hand-carved paddle with deep strokes as he towed the net backward out into the current. His wooden floats, carved in the shape of birds, and his small stone or ivory weights would have slipped off the deck of his kayak until he reached the end of the net and dropped a stone anchor.

I owed much of my overactive imagination to the woman crafting willow chairs while waiting for us at fish camp. That was my mom, an educator and perpetual student of indigenous cultures and history. Her teaching job had brought our family to the river when I was a kid. We'd left the cowboy country of Montana when I was in second grade for the tundra and winding rivers of southwestern Alaska.

Lost in thought, I barely noticed the floats already beginning to dip and jerk.

"I hope that's not a snag there," my dad said, snapping me from my daydream. He pointed toward the middle of our set, where the floatline appeared to be sinking. The sight of the now partially submerged floats was disconcerting. We had borrowed the net from family friends, and it wouldn't look good if we lost such an essential food-gathering asset to a submerged log on our first drift of the summer.

Our concern for the net shifted as a huge king salmon slammed the line and thrashed right at the top, flipping up and casting a mist that showered both of us. The thick broad tail arched out of the water and slapped down against the surface like some sort of miniature river whale. Then another king hit high in the column. Thrashing. Then another.

The net wasn't caught against a submerged spruce log; it was caught against a school of swimming salmon logs. Kuskokwim kings.

I turned away from the splashing toward my dad working at the stern. I'd thought we'd be spending a leisurely day drifting down the river, bringing home a dozen kings to smoke and freeze. Instead, concern mounted with each passing second. I didn't even have time to ask how long we should wait. He was yelling, "Start pulling or we'll be in trouble!"

Of course I'd grown up hearing stories of people catching too many fish while out commercial fishing and sinking their boat when the wind came up, so that thought flashed through my mind, but I knew the real trouble he was talking about would be the work of processing a boatload of giant kings.

The entire net hadn't been in the water more than a minute, and I was already leaning over the cold metal bow and pulling for my life. The thing didn't seem to budge at first. If anything, the net came alive and pulled back against me like a recoil rope on an old boat engine. I groaned and heaved and began pulling with everything I had. My dad killed the motor and crawled over the empty fish tote and a beat-up blue cooler. He snatched up the floatline. The work began.

The first king, thick as my thigh, came flying over the gunwale. The others joining this fat fellow on our boat's floorboards were even bigger. We seemed to have snared some sort of salmon dynasty. Big, beautiful, silvery behemoths rained from the water and up and into the bow of our little skiff. My forearms and back ached from the strain, and we gave up untangling the fish and poured our efforts into getting the net in before we plugged the mesh that remained in the water. The longer the net soaked, the more fish hit. And we didn't need or want any more.

Finally, I reached down and yanked the last of the line from the river. The final king in the eight-inch mesh, caught just by the edge of a gill, shook free, and seemed to drift there for a moment alongside the boat. I lowered my arm to grab it but instead ran my hand down the length of its enormous body. We had more than enough, but here was this giant king within reach, the top spines of its long dorsal fin barely breaking the river's smooth surface. When would I have another chance to grab a beauty like that with my bare hands? The king seemed to be waiting for me to snatch its tail and heave it into the boat. I waited a moment longer, brushing my hand against the scales, unsure if the fish would survive the trauma of the net. Then, with the flick of its powerful tail, the salmon disappeared like living quicksilver into the mud-colored water.

On the ride back through the slough to our fish camp that early June day in 1989 I tried to count the big heads as they slid around with each wave and sharp turn of the boat. I kept losing count, and it wouldn't be until we pulled to shore and started lugging them up the beach that we'd get the final count. Thirty-seven in a drift that lasted mere minutes. I was ready to get back to town and tell my friends how we caught all the kings in that one quick drift.

What I remember distinctly was that feeling of amazement that the river and those kings could provide so much sustenance and happiness for so many. We arrived at camp with far more salmon than our family of five would need and enough for us to share with countless other friends and a few elders. One widow greeted me at the door of her house in town and, in the excitement for her first fresh king of the year, took both me and the fish into her arms with a big hug and a soft whisper of thanks I can still hear.

It never occurred to me that I would never again, in my lifetime, see king fishing like that.

I don't think anyone thought fishing would ever be much different, there in southwestern Alaska. We didn't take the gift of the salmon for granted, not ever, but we were all guilty of taking their existence for granted. Not one of us there at our fish camp, the other camps lining the river for miles, or in boats drifting for king salmon that summer would have imagined that in the coming years the kings, those beautiful monsters of the salmon family, might not return.

Or perhaps we'd only hoped that the fish would always be there, despite what the Yup'ik elders said. Those sages of the tundra had been warning us for years that as people grew more disrespectful, greedy, and violent, the earth would follow suit and change for the worse, in terms of climate and a sustainable home for us. The phrase they used is *ella-gguq yun'i maliggluku cimirtuq,* which means "the earth is changing following its people." The elders cautioned that disrespect for the Yup'ik rules about how to live, mistreatment of the animals, and being wasteful would lead to degradation in the environment and loss of fish and land animals. Those of us who grew up along the Kuskokwim heard their constant cautions about the looming changes in the earth and animal behavior and populations, but none of us took those warnings seriously enough.

The truth is we were all too consumed with consuming. When it came just to fishing, we wanted bigger and faster boats, longer nets, and longer commercial fishing periods. More fish equaled more money to purchase more gear to catch more fish. Fishing was the one and only industry on the river. The salmon were plentiful and the admonishments of the elders were lost in the din of progress and profit.

It turns out they were right.

I know of no other people on the planet who rely so deeply on salmon in their diets as the Yup'ik people. Salmon have always been essential to their survival, and the culture is deeply connected to the fish and the water. Traditional beliefs and behaviors have for millennia revolved around respect for this source of life.

A powerful example is revealed in Yup'ik cosmology. Animals, including salmon, give themselves to the people. Upon taking the life of a creature the hunter or fisherman gives thanks directly to that animal. Rules are in place regarding everything from how to clean it and prepare the meat to how to dispose of bones. Every step in the process of hunting and fishing revolves around respect for the animal and the land from which it came. Disrespecting a creature, even after it has been killed, could have devastating results for an entire community. Wasting a single salmon, for example, could mean that fish and his kin might choose to never return, and the whole village might starve as a result.

To the casual observer, this belief system may appear as nothing more than a strange superstition, but perhaps there is deep and abiding wisdom buried in the ancient practice. Distilled to its essence, the custom reveals a powerful relationship between humanity and the ecosystem, and therein lies the most important lesson for us all: giving thanks to the fish that give themselves to us is a way for us all to save the salmon and ourselves.

I first learned of this concept during the winter of second grade. We lived in the village of Akiak at the time, and Robert Ivan, a respected hunter and musher, had taken me under his wing. The two of us left the village by dogteam to check his *taluyaq*, a "fish trap." When we pulled the large contraption from beneath the ice, I thought at first it looked like a space capsule crafted from bent willows. Robert said little to nothing on most of our outings, but when he did speak, I knew it was usually something he really thought I needed to know. That day there were only a few fish in the trap. A couple of whitefish, and one big fat burbot as long and thick as my two-year-old sister. I'd never seen such an exotic animal. The eel-like creature slithered around inside the trap until Robert grabbed it and thrust it toward me for me to add it to the sled's basket. He said, simply, "We say *quyana* to these fish that share with us," and he waited for me to repeat the word of thanks.

"*Quyana,*" I said.

Twenty-five years have passed since my dad and I caught our last great haul of Kuskokwim kings, and now I fight back tears and swallow hard at what feels like a dry chunk of overbaked salmon lodged deep in my throat. I may never share such an incredible experience with Atticus, my three-year-old son. The numbers of kings in the Kuskokwim and all around Alaska are dwindling, and the kings seem to be shrinking in size, too. Restrictions are in place along the river to allow for escapement, but there are vast commercial fishing threats at sea, the climate is changing, and a massive new mine is planned in the watershed, midway up the Kuskokwim River. On the Kuskokwim and elsewhere in Alaska, the days with drying racks and tender boats laden with salmon are no more.

We must endeavor to find a way to stop thinking a successful day of fishing is catching all we can carry, and instead be happy and grateful with a few less fish caught today, so there will be *more* for tomorrow.

I no longer live on the Kuskokwim, but I consider it home and plan to spend many summer days with my son on that incredible river. I hope my stories of netting giant king salmon with his grandpa don't seem like old made-up fish stories to him, akin to my own grandpa's stories of pistol-packing cowboys roping grizzlies for fun and harvesting mountainous piles of buffalo bones for fertilizer when he was a boy. More important, I want him to know the joy a big fish gives an elder when he brings it to her door. I also want him to know and understand that Yup'ik notion of respect for *ella*, "the earth," her fish, and all the creatures.

For my son's sake, and for all of us, I wish we could look back at the traditional Yup'ik approach and realize the solution to saving the salmon resides with our children learning from birth the importance of respect. Perhaps if we teach that concept of *ella-gguq yun'i maliggluku cimirtuq* to our kids and empower them to protect and respect the fish, the world *will* change, on its own terms, and hopefully in a way that is positive for all the creatures.

For now, I'm haunted by the big king floating at my fingertips. I'll never forget that day of fishing on the Kuskokwim with my dad or that final flash of the king's broad tail, a fleeting glimpse of silver disappearing into the dark river's silty depths.

Just as salmon return to the beaches of Bristol Bay, so does my family. My generation is the fourth to return to our fish camp every year. Now that everyone's getting older we have a fifth generation to teach. Fish camp is where I hold some of my most prized childhood memories. To see little ones running around camp, learning how to fish and live, fills my heart with pure joy. I think back to my late grandfather and I know this is exactly how he wanted it to be. When he taught us how to fish, he gave us life. No matter how far away any of us live, we return just as the fish do, one by one, every year.

Tatiana Petticrew
South Naknek

Growing up in Unalakleet In the 1970s and '80s was an amazing time for our family. We would spend days cutting hundreds of fish throughout the summer. We started with the mighty king salmon, savoring the first king of the year along with the king crab we caught. Then our eyes turned toward netting enough kings to turn them into smoked strips. On a good year we'd cut forty to fifty kings. After the kings we'd turn our attention to pink salmon. This is where we'd spend a weekend at a time cutting hundreds of pinks to dry for our year's worth of dried fish. Our families would gather upriver on a sandbar and seine for the pinks. After pinks, we'd start on silver salmon. The silver salmon was the fish we'd freeze whole or in fillets. Finally we'd fish for the late fall silvers for drying and for the caviar. We'd eagerly wait for the eggs that were ready to spawn, squeeze the eggs out of the fish, and have caviar on crackers washed down with Tang.

Thinking back, my mother was an amazing person to have the wherewithal to preserve many types of fish for the whole year. We'd have smoked strips, canned fish, salted fish for pickling, fermented fish heads, fermented eggs, caviar, frozen salmon, both pink salmon and late fall silver salmon for dried fish.

Today we do some of the same, but not quite as many.

Paul Ivanoff
Unalakleet

My Salmon Project

MICHAEL RAUDZIS DINKEL

Michael Raudzis Dinkel is a writer, artist, and wood-carver currently living in Anchorage. He studied art and creative writing at the University of Alaska Anchorage and at St. John's University in Collegeville, Minnesota. His most recent work is a mail-art project that combines essay and images to address the degradation of salmon habitat in Alaska.

IT DOESN'T MATTER HOW MUCH I LOVE SALMON, or appreciate their life journeys into the North Pacific and back, I have always fished them with numbers in my head. This was understandable when I was gillnetting. I thought about the price per pound and added up my fish tickets; I needed to count dollars. I had a payment to make, crew and nets to pay for, and I needed to make enough money for the winter. This attitude persisted into my sportfishing; I wanted my limit, usually at least three reds or silvers a day for my freezer. I fished diligently until I had what I considered enough.

These days I've been going to the Kenai River to dipnet my red salmon in the personal-use fishery. With two people in our household, my wife and I can take thirty-five fish. I count them off as I catch them. This produces a lot of vacuum-packed fillets, but to take less than the full amount seems like failure. I know this because last summer I miscounted and came home with thirty-four. Even though I already had more than we needed, that last fish nagged at me, wherever it had gone off to.

It was that missing number thirty-five that started me thinking about salmon on a fish-by-fish basis. Because of the perceived abundance of these fish and the large limits allowed, I think that I need more than I do. It is one of the things that erode the common respect most of us have for what these creatures really are. I began to wonder how many fish I really should take, and if I was being careless about the ones I did get. Would I need as many if I tried to use more of each one? It seemed like a place to start; later I could rearrange my ideas about how many fish I really wanted. I didn't want to fret anymore about how many I could catch, or the overly generous number I am allowed, but how many I should ethically catch.

I thought about what happens when I land a fresh sockeye on the beach. It is always exciting, even with a dipnet. That sleek red muscle covered with silver, carrying the North Pacific into the Kenai River. Or maybe chrome is a better word; or the color of water and light in that perfect shape. The fish is all life and desperate to get back into the river. It is hard and bright and twisting and swirling with all its strength. Then I put the club to it. A couple of solid smacks, a tightening shudder, and it becomes a different thing. I have taken its life. I want to think this dying fish, the blood leaking from its gills, now belongs to me.

I felt like I needed to take more responsibility for this possession, what a salmon becomes when I catch it and kill it, when it is dead. It's not a fish anymore, or it's a dead fish and I think of ice, my knife, what is the best thing to do with it now that it's my food.

If I was going to keep fewer and use more of these fish, I had to work out a new way to process them. I needed to do it differently from when I was in a hurry to get as many as possible. This time I kept the roe from the females, the milt from the males, and livers from all of them. I cut the fillets into smaller portions than I had in the past. I also saved the collars and bellies, something I had considered optional in the past on days when I had a lot of fish to clean. I kept the heads for fish head soup along with the tails and backbones. All of this changed how and when I cleaned them, and it took more time. I soon found that I would need more ice and separate containers for each of the parts.

I felt like I was at the beginning of a new adventure. Even after the thousands of salmon I had harvested in my past, I began to see something new. The roe was the first of it; I learned to cure the eggs into salmon caviar. With this I discovered some of the most beautiful food I have ever eaten. I ate them lightly salted on crackers or on my scrambled eggs at breakfast. I found someone who remembered how my wife Karen's grandmother made fish head soup. The backbones went into the pot with the heads, taking advantage of the occasionally botched filleting job. I've always known the collars and bellies were special with their extra fat; these I smoked separately after grilling some of them until the skin was crisp. I didn't have as much success with the milt and the livers, so I have something to work on next summer.

So did I learn how many fish two people can reasonably consume in a year? I'm still figuring that one out. But there was another unexpected result of my endeavors. All of that intimate delving into the salmon's body—the careful egg taking, the milt, collecting livers, considering the head with its fat behind the eye, the nutritious brain, and cheek meat—all of this brought an unexpected connection. While I was being careful with each fish, new feelings of gratitude and compassion began to accompany my actions. Seeing the fish as more than two fillets, looking inside of it and caring for the eggs and heads let me see what I had in my hands. Once beautiful and silver and alive with the sea in its belly and the history of the Kenai River in its life, it was now bringing me into its story and giving me a personal connection to it. I couldn't see this when I was grabbing for that handful off the top and thoughtlessly taking more than my portion.

I think of salmon today as a gift more than a given. A gift implies thankfulness. My experiment did more than help us decide how many fish we could use in our household; it added to the changing way I am thinking about fish and the river. A more intense use of each individual fish made me more aware of these salmon outside of the frame I had always looked into when it was time to catch them. It's the opposite of the big picture, the other end of it, and the place where it touches us. It doesn't have to be fish head soup or milt sautéed in garlic butter but just a change in the idea of salmon, the ones that come to us and the ones that swim past. Both might benefit from a new story.

At every turn I hear scientists discussing the future of this resource. I know salmon need science to survive the future we're making here in Alaska, but science can give us the illusion that we might be able to sidestep some of the responsibilities connected to these fish and their homes, our homes. It can even make us think we can fix what we damage and ignore the things these fish need to remain themselves and not our version of what they are. Salmon can also benefit from a way that is separate from science. For me, using more of the fish gave me a way to make the others, the living ones, more immediate and important. There were even moments when I felt a partnership with them and this place, an awareness of how much it means to me to have them in our lives and what it will take to have a salmon future.

Every summer, families went to fish camps as soon as the river ice flowed out, or others left early in spring before the ice got soft. The men would leave for the cannery in Kenai while we dried our fish in camps, and they would join us later. I remember a day when a very strong wind came and our wall tents were blowing like tissue paper. We children gathered near our moms to brave the high winds. I remember too, the rows of wall tents along the river. We are truly the people of the land, gatherers of the bounty that our higher power provides. I'm blessed to understand and live in that earthly connection: the fresh salmon we crave by spring that sees us through winter. This fish is gold to me.

Eva O'Malley
Anchorage

I started fishing salmon in 1962, and Snug Harbor on Chisik Island became my home port. Joe Fribrock was the owner of the cannery and was always so nice to me. I started with his worst boat which was the *Not So Snug*. It was only twenty-eight feet and had no hydraulics. Yes, I pulled the net by hand. Also, nobody in those days had deckhands. We fished alone. After the first year, Joe could tell that I had the makings of a fisherman so he upgraded the boat that I would fish each year. I loved it so much that I was a top fisherman for them year after year. I fished salmon in Cook Inlet for nearly fifty years and had a total love affair with it.

When the corridor was implemented, my love was turning into an angry heart, so I gave it up. To this day I long to go out there and fish twenty-four hours a day, three days a week or more, and fish anywhere in the inlet. No doubt, those were the days.

Jerre Wills
Homer

Give Me a Life Jacket and a Paddle

HEATHER LENDE

Heather Lende is the author of *If You Lived Here, I'd Know Your Name* and a former contributing editor for *Woman's Day* magazine. She lives in Haines, Alaska.

POET MARY OLIVER WROTE that what we must do with the only wild and precious life we have is simple: pay attention, be astonished, and tell about it. I am, by temperament and experience, prepared to be inspired by the simple gifts of this particular mid-February morning in my favorite place— the beach out my back door where the Chilkat River meets the sea. It is a lot better than watching over my shoulder for a truck that may hit me.

Once, on a later spring morning than this one, I saw a man run down this beach in cycling shorts and rubber boots. He splashed through the icy channels and grabbed a big king salmon marooned on the low-tide flats. He got to it as the eagles were circling in. A woman with a wheelbarrow chased after him. With hands bloodied by reaching into the fish's mouth and grabbing the jaw to lift it, he said, "I forgot fish had teeth" and dropped the thirty-pounder into the wheelbarrow. The two of them pushed it down the beach after he made me promise not to tell anyone, since he wasn't sure if his sportfishing license applied to a salmon caught without a hook. The man reasoned that he hadn't caught the salmon at all. He had *found* it. Later he paid me off with a delicious chunk for my dinner.

There are times late at night when I wonder if it was dishonest to eat that fish. If I was too greedy. There is nothing better after a winter of eating out of the freezer than fresh king salmon with a squirt of lemon. But what if everyone grabbed one like that? Not that we all could, and it is uncommon to see one beached, but still. Should I have told him to push it back into the current? Aren't we humans the only species who have the ability to both destroy and maintain life? Shouldn't we lean toward the latter, always? I asked him about it the next time I saw him. "The fish was a goner either way," he said. "He'd been stuck too long. The birds would have gotten him is all." Which made me feel better, sort of. "You worry too much," he said.

I do worry. I worry because I know it is warmer than it used to be. February feels like April. I heard on the news that this is the hottest year ever recorded on Earth. I turn off the lights when I leave the room and use cloth grocery bags, but what is one woman, a grandmother no less, to do?

On today's morning walk there's nothing as morally challenging, or as interesting, as a handsome man in cycling shorts. Instead, there is a humbling grandeur—I apologize, but that's the word for it. If I took a photograph you'd think it was fake. The winter-white mountains, the fog, and the wide thawing mudflats in the silver light all combine for an Ansel Adams–style image that could be Yosemite at the beach. It is the sort of dawn when all is right with the world. If I see my fisherman friend JR walking his dogs, he'll say in his Bronx accent, "I wonder what the rich people are looking at this morning."

But it's just my dog and me out here. I pick up a heart-shaped stone. Breathe in the low-tide new-seaweed ozone scent that is proof that spring will arrive as surely as the hooligan and king salmon that will run the river in a few months.

When May comes it will charge up the Chilkat like a battle of bands. The fish and their entourage of sea lions, seals, and shorebirds will all soon be singing to the backbeat of the melting streams and rising river, bears black and brown splashing for breakfast, the distant (and not so distant) thunder from avalanches, and the sweet hoo-hooing of the grouse. From May's hooligan and king salmon tango until early winter's eagle ball in Klukwan, it's one big sold-out show after another, the rest of the salmon—sockeye, pinks, chum, and coho—following the kings. The Chilkat concert season ends in late November and early December with a grand finale of the largest gathering of bald eagles in the world. Some three thousand annually descend on the snowy river flats near Klukwan to feed on what's left of the spawning chums concentrated in naturally occurring warm pools in the otherwise frozen river twenty miles upstream from where I stand.

Everyone and everything is part of this ancient and modern song and dance. The people, the fish, the place. In Klukwan they chant the stories and drum with the spirits of the animals and fish guiding them. We all eat salmon, and some of us make a living catching them. My neighbor Gregg, who has gillnetted for salmon for about forty years, bangs on a banjo in a band called the Fishpickers, and he plays bridge with an old gold miner at seven every winter Thursday in the Catholic Church basement. They are great friends, so they avoid talk of a new copper, zinc, silver, and gold mine still in the exploratory phase at the headwaters of the Chilkat. The processes of mining and smelting can't be good for rivers and salmon.

Is there such a thing as worrying too much? So much depends on salmon survival. People I love, for starters. Gregg's daughter is married to another neighbor's son. Frank runs his own salmon power troller. Two doors down from Frank's dad's boat shop is Betty's house, and another big old boat shed. Her husband, Don, was a fisherman too, and he also built beautiful and practical gillnetters. Their only son drowned with three other Haines kids when his boat sank in a storm. Betty told me that when a child dies you lose your future. My son is a commercial fisherman, and so is one son-in-law. Another son-in-law is a fisheries biologist; he doesn't have to remind me that if we lose the salmon in our river, Haines and Klukwan will lose some—maybe all—of our children to other places and other ways of life. It would be so quiet here without them. And without the Fishpickers swinging on a Saturday night at the Pioneer Bar.

Another New England poet, Emily Dickinson, wrote that life is sweeter because it doesn't last forever. It should be easier to understand that when your house looks out on a river where all five species of Pacific salmon spawn and die. You don't need to be a poet to recognize the living metaphor of birth, death, and—each spring when the fry depart for the nurturing sea—rebirth. But even though I sing, "Time, like an ever rolling stream, bears all our years away" in church, I'm not always comforted.

I would love to tell you that on this watercolor kind of morning I am as much a part of the scene as that weathered white jawbone of last summer's salmon stuck in the tide line detritus, a few of its teeth still attached, and that the raven's cry didn't startle me a minute ago. I would like to be as tuned in to this day and this place as a poet or a priest or a Tlingit elder from long ago. I have eaten my weight in salmon every year for the past thirty. My Native neighbors would say my very flesh and blood should be mostly salmon by now, which should make me part of all this too, right?

Yet this morning I missed a wolf. A wolf! I have never heard of a wolf on this side of the river. When I got home my husband said it was standing on the beach at Pyramid Island. Pearl and I walked within stick-tossing distance of a large black wolf and never suspected we had company. I am a total failure in the mindful-walking department. You'd think the dog would have at least caught his scent. This is why I'm not a nature writer. My attention wanders. I daydream. I'm too astonished.

Once, I thought I might try to write about life and death in the wild and some profound, good lesson I learned after witnessing a cow moose swim and wade toward the island with a relatively newborn calf. A bear had chased them into the river. When she came to a deep channel she tucked the little one underneath her torso, its nose a snorkel poking up between her hind legs. I watched the drama through binoculars from a wheelchair while my family ate pancakes. I had no appetite, thanks to the morphine, which was needed to dull the pain from a smashed pelvis, the result of a truck driver not noticing me pedaling down the quiet street that he drove on every day on his way home for lunch. He even stopped at the intersection and looked both ways before he ran right over me.

I believed that witnessing the cow and calf fight for their lives with so much unknown about my prognosis was a sign that I, too, should not give up.

When my husband said the cow was on the island, we clapped.

Then he said, "I don't see the calf at all. She keeps looking back."

Finally he said, "The calf didn't make it."

I was so sad I couldn't talk. But there is enough woe in the world already without me making my family feel worse than they already did. Aren't we all swimming upstream to an unknown fate? Life is too precious to waste it complaining. I asked my daughter to wheel me over to the hospital bed tucked into the front window.

I thanked her and closed my eyes.

Which is a long way of saying that these days the joy I find in walking my dog in this wonderful world is plenty. My good fortune—call it luck or grace—slays me. I certainly don't deserve this ending any more than that baby moose deserved its. It is a new day and thank God I am in it. That's why I was humming show tunes in the fog when I totally missed the wolf. It's not that I wasn't paying attention. I was celebrating.

The wolf was still out there when another dog walker came by that morning. We hailed her from the porch and helped her to see him. Then her dog barked and the wolf howled. Bark and howl repeated as we listened until the wolf trotted out of sight.

Pearl and I joined Margaret for the rest of her walk. She's the news director at the radio station, was imbedded with the troops in Iraq, and can bake Twinkies from scratch. "Is a wolf news?" I asked.

"Maybe," Margaret said.

News is when things don't go as planned. News is when a person leaves home on a bike ride and is hit by a truck and doesn't return for two months.

It is *not* news when she cycles along the road next to this river twenty-one miles to Klukwan, the Tlingit village that has been there since time immemorial, as the elders say. The mother village of the Chilkat people. One translation of Chilkat is "large basket of fish." My eggs are all in this basket and, as Mark Twain said, I better be watching it. It holds the two grandchildren next door, two more across town, my children, my husband, my neighbors and favorite fishermen, the beach where the mighty Chilkat meets the sea, and the perfect cookout in July when fresh sockeye is grilled over a driftwood fire and there's new lettuce and strawberries in a salad from the garden. The children are sunburned, the dogs are all wet, and the run is above average. If that basket spills or is stolen it will be news, but too late to save the precious contents.

Margaret and I decided if nothing else more newsworthy came up that day in our small town, a possibility for sure, the wolf could make the evening report. "Can I call you for a quote?" she asked. I thought, if she does, will I have the courage to say that I think the wolf was trying to tell us to pay attention to the weird weather and to a potential mine of a type that I can't even pronounce, a mine that straddles a tributary named Klehini, "Mothers' Water"?

The local stories that endure long past the daily news cycle, thousands of years even, teach that the first people to live in the Chilkat Valley walked from the Interior and came to the backside of these glacier-covered mountains only to be hemmed into an alpine valley by walls of ice. Water from one glacier was backing up, flooding the valley floor. They couldn't stay there long. There was water running under another glacier down a kind of tunnel. Some of the young men thought they could scale the peaks and climb out, but the families couldn't, the babies and old people especially could not, and the mothers would not leave their children.

And here the migration tale takes different paths depending on who is telling it, but since I am, I will share the version I imagine. A grandmother volunteers to ride in the canoe down that waterfall under that glacier. She knows she could die, or find a route through the mountains to a new home for her children's children and beyond. She is old and has nothing—and everything—to lose if she doesn't try it. She climbs into the canoe. The people sing a song and say a prayer and push her off. She closes her eyes and holds on tight and with an "I love you" is gone. Before she knows what has happened, the canoe skids onto a beach. She is afraid to look. She hears the Chilkat Valley spring symphony of hooligan and salmon. Hope floats her heart higher in her chest, and she opens her eyes and sees a perfect May day—more or less the same as we still do—with sparkling ocean and river, blue sky, tall spruce trees, and the green haze of budding alder, cottonwood, and birch. King salmon leap in the waves, hawks hover over voles scurrying in the grass, goats trip along a cliff. She reckons she has died, but the afterlife is better than she had dreamed. She sneezes. She must be alive if she can't find her hankie. She is sure it was in her tunic pocket when she left. She sees a young man from her clan looking down from a mountain, so she jumps up and waves with both arms. Her people raft down to join her.

I owe that old woman. Two of my granddaughters are related to those long-ago settlers, maybe even to her directly. I feed them salmon from this river, salmon I've smoked in alder the same way she did.

The other day I was walking on the beach with Margaret's husband, John, who is a salmon gillnetter and a descendent of another tribe who settled farther north. He said that his grandmother was one of three survivors of a Spanish flu epidemic that killed all but three babies in her home village of about two thousand souls. Relatives far from that place reared her.

Even I couldn't imagine the grief. "I'm just grateful that I inherited her immune system. I never get sick," John said. On Thanksgiving he eats turkey like the pilgrims who nearly wiped his lineage out. "It's problematic," he says, because he does have so much to be thankful for.

When I came from a Seattle nursing home, broken-bodied and afraid I'd never walk again, and my children and mother-in-law helped me into that bed by the window; it was also May. They had remembered to put the screens in, and the sashes were up. You can tell me it was the narcotics talking, but I swear that the music of the river and the salmon swimming up it in that steady, eternal way rafted my spirit to health. The river didn't bear all my cares away, but it made them bearable.

I can climb the stairs to my own room now, and I love waking up here more than ever. But sometimes in December, when mornings are so dark, I stay under the quilt with Pearl at my feet, listening to the radio news, and feel a weight pressing on my heart. Especially when it's raining and it should be snowing.

I saw that calf die. I didn't see the wolf right next to me. I had a truck run me over and was nearly killed because the driver wasn't paying attention. He meant no harm. Then, I prayed I would live to see grandchildren I didn't even know I had yearned for. None of my children were even married. Ten years later I have five grandchildren that I love so fiercely it astonishes me. But I missed that wolf in plain sight. What if it had charged Pearl, or worse—if I had been with one of the children and it had rabies or something? What if he decided a howl wasn't enough to get our attention? What about that mine? I must pay more attention and tell about it.

It is not enough to fall on my knees with my face to the setting sun as the wild and precious salmon push hard for home, and to pray: *O salmon, O river, O air we breathe and water we drink, forgive us for what we have done and what we have left undone,* the way my mother taught me, and hand God the helm. I knew a great-grandmother named Belle who crossed out what she called the "royal we" in her prayers replacing it with her name. Heather, what have you done? Heather, what have you left undone? I hear the ghost voice of a dear departed elder, a rosy-cheeked, white-bearded fisherman, a Haines native with a small *n*, say "Speak for the fish, Heather, and the rest will take care of itself."

Every year since my mother died, I type and edit my father's Christmas letter from handwritten faxes sent from his Hudson Valley farm. He is eighty-one and won't use a computer. In this year's letter, Dad wrote about how he was the oldest person to complete the annual Hudson River crossing, a two-mile swim sponsored by Pete Seeger to celebrate cleaning up a river that was once too toxic to dip his face in. "You can eat the fish again in some places," Dad said over the phone. Just before wishing everyone a happy holiday season and joyous New Year, he had me type, "The Earth is on fire and the only strong leader on the world stage is a Russian gangster." I suggested it was a tad negative for a Christmas card. He was eating his supper and spoke with his mouth full. He calls at dinnertime now that he is alone. He lights a candle, sets the table, heats up some soup, and puts me on speakerphone. He chewed a minute, took a sip of his wine, and said, "Heath, I have to say something and the fuckers are killing us."

What is a good daughter, mother, and grandmother to do? Sit in her rocker knitting like Madame Defarge, shrieking that the end is near and it's everyone else's fault, from Chinese coal plants to Canadian mining companies, swear like a sailor and chug her evening Pinot straight from the bottle, because we are all going to die anyway?

Please hand me a life jacket because I've volunteered to take a boat under a glacier down a waterfall, even though I get motion sickness, am afraid of the dark, have never done any whitewater paddling in my life, and I know I should be better at recycling. I'll bring Pearl and some dry fish from Klukwan, a potted geranium, and a tin of organic, non-GMO flour cookies. I will get a flu shot before I leave and make sure that I'm not wearing any toxic beauty products. My Tlingit son-in-law can carve me a paddle. John will shove me off for good luck. He's proof that a people can come back from the brink. Maybe Dad will join me. He has a wetsuit and is a good swimmer.

I would do that much to save the one precious and wild home I have. Wouldn't you? What the heck are we waiting for?